Essential
New
Orleans

by

HONEY NAYLOR

When not travel writing around the world,
Honey Naylor's favourite occupation
is to write about her home town
of New Orleans.
She is a contributor to Fodor's *Florida* and
author of Fodor's *New Orleans*.

Produced by the Publishing Division of
The Automobile Association

Written by Honey Naylor
Peace and Quiet section by Paul
Sterry
Consultant: Frank Dawes

Edited, designed and produced by
the Publishing Division of The
Automobile Association 1990.
Maps © The Automobile
Association 1990.

Distributed in the United Kingdom
by the Publishing Division of The
Automobile Association, Fanum
House, Basingstoke, Hampshire,
RG21 2EA.

A CIP catalogue record for this book
is available from the British Library.

ISBN 0 86145 870 2

Published by The Automobile
Association.

Typesetting: Avonset, Midsomer
Norton, Bath.
Colour separation: L C Repro,
Aldermaston.
Printing: Printers S.R.L., Trento,
Italy.

Front cover picture:
a Louisiana riverboat

This book employs a
simple rating system to
help choose which
places to visit:

◆◆◆   do not miss

◆◆   see if you can

◆   worth seeing if
      you have time

INTRODUCTION

New Orleans is a misfit. The Big Easy, as it is called – and you will understand why as soon as you arrive – is a displaced city with a mood more akin to the Mediterranean than North America. It sits right on the Mississippi

A city of contrasts: New Orleans, the biggest city in Louisiana, has a brash, modern face and a lively history

River, 110 miles (177km) inland from the Gulf of Mexico, and somehow seems about to drift downriver until it reaches some spot in the Caribbean where it could bask in the sun and take things even easier than it already does. You can sense the easy-going ambience of the city immediately. Many visitors say they feel life's tensions slip away as soon as they step off the plane. With its subtropical climate and laid-back pace, this really is 'the city that care forgot' – another of New Orleans' several sobriquets.

The climate – steamy in the summer, with heavy moisture-laden air – produces a profusion of rich vegetation: magnificent magnolia trees with glossy, dark green leaves and snow-white blossoms; banana plants with broad, pale green fronds. Tall palms, squat palms, palms of almost every variety grow here, along with majestic, centuries-old oaks covered in tangled grey beards of Spanish moss. In the spring, the city is awash with brilliant azaleas, wisteria, oleanders, bougainvillea and roses.

Even the sounds of the city are easy-going: the long, low moan of sea-going vessels saluting each other as they glide in and out of one of the world's largest ports; riverboat calliopes, wheezy and off-key, alerting everyone that it's time to board for a lazy cruise up and down Old Man River; and the slow, steady clip-clop of the long-eared mules that pull fringed carriages full of tourists through the French Quarter.

New Orleanians adore their legends. You hear so much about voodoo queen Marie Laveau, pirate Jean Lafitte, Andrew Jackson, and Napoleon that you almost expect to turn a corner and bump into one of them. Lafitte's Blacksmith Shop and the Napoleon House are two favoured French Quarter watering holes, fine places to spend an entire afternoon doing nothing but soaking up the atmosphere and enjoying life.

Napoleon, of course, never set foot in New Orleans, but he had many supporters here. Today, the Napoleon House looks near collapse, but when Napoleon was exiled on St Helena it was the stately mansion of New

Orleans Mayor Nicholas Girod. According to legend, Girod organized a syndicate to rescue the Little Corporal. The top floor of his house was to be Napoleon's home. A schooner was dispatched to fetch him, but Napoleon died before it arrived.

The schooner, so it is said, was commanded by one of Jean Lafitte's freebooters. Lafitte is one of history's most mysterious characters. He is said to have been a swashbuckling pirate, a slave-trader, and a smuggler who used the blacksmith shop on Bourbon Street as a front for illegal activities. No evidence exists that the weatherbeaten cottage was ever a blacksmith shop. But, like the Napoleon House, the place oozes atmosphere.

Mardi Gras, the biggest festival in North America, is a marvellous mixture of myth, magic, make-believe, food, parties, and flat-out fun. And it is only the largest of a year-round calendar of festivals in this 24-hour party town. New Orleans has annual festivals honouring the French Quarter, Louis Armstrong, adopted son Tennessee Williams, spring, food, jazz, classical music, and Christ. New Orleans party animals even celebrate new additions to the Audubon Zoo.

Jazz always plays a part in the festivities. Jazz was born in New Orleans, a child created of Afro-Caribbean rhythms, European brass bands, spirituals and 'jubilees' sung in black churches, ragtime, and even the sing-song sound of old-time street vendors.

ARKANSAS

MISSISSIPPI

TEXAS

LOUISIANA

New Orleans

Gulf of Mexico

The people of New Orleans are as much a part of the city's character as its narrow streets and balconied buildings

BACKGROUND

The very first festival here might simply have celebrated survival. Life for the earliest settlers was harsh; many were lured here under false pretences, in one of history's great land frauds. An 18th-century Scotsman named John Law made his way into the French Court and obtained a 25-year charter to exploit the Louisiana Territory, which had earlier been claimed for Louis XIV. In 1717, Law ordered French Creoles, who had already established other colonies in the Territory, to establish a settlement on the Mississippi River. (A Creole was a word

originally used to designate a full-blooded
child born in the colony; these days it means
anything indigenous to this region, from a
tomato to a lady.) Law christened the new
colony La Nouvelle Orléans, after the duc
d'Orléans, regent to the child king Louis XV.
He then papered Europe with broadsides
proclaiming the great wealth to be found in
the New World.

The Europeans who arrived found, instead, a
wealth of problems. Hurricanes, hostile
Indians, floods, yellow fever, and a few
French Creoles living in crude palmetto huts.
Having given up home and hearth, the
newcomers had little choice but to dig in and
survive.

New Orleans grew from a tough waterfront
settlement to a Crown Colony, and life here
took on many of the characteristics of the
glittering French Court. The city soon gained
a reputation as a 'good-time town.' There
were grand balls, salons and soirées. It was
also a place teeming with freebooters,
voodoo practitioners, and all sorts of unusual
characters.

In 1762, to the horror of the French Creoles,
France ceded the colony to Spain. According
to one story, Louis XV had lost a bet to his
cousin, Charles III of Spain, and paid off his
debt with the entire Louisiana Territory. Riots
broke out in protest, but the Spanish quelled
them, took control, and ruled for more than 30
years. By and large, the only Spaniards who
arrived here were the government officials,
and the city remained a French Creole
colony.

During the Spanish period, two disastrous
fires swept through the town. In 1788, the
entire colony was destroyed except for one
structure, the Old Ursuline Convent on
Chartres Street. Again, in 1794, a terrible fire
broke out, but much of the rebuilt colony was
spared. As a result, although the French
Quarter's spirit may be Gallic, its architecture
now has a hint of Spanish. During the
rebuilding, much of the French Creole
character was retained, but there are definite
Spanish flourishes.

It was during the Spanish era that the Cajuns

A Creole cottage in the Garden District, a residential area which came to boast some of the most elegant and elaborate mansions in the city

arrived in this part of the world. In the early 17th century, French colonists had settled in what is now Nova Scotia and called their colony l'Acadie. In the mid-18th century the Acadians – Cajuns is a corruption of the word – were expelled, and many of the exiles found their way to South Louisiana. The Spanish gave them land grants, and they settled in southwest Louisiana, the cradle of the Cajun style, which has swept this country and others as well. This is a great place to visit, and deserves a couple of days at least to do it justice. The Cajun slogan is: *Laissez les bons temps rouler,* or 'Let the good times roll' – a phrase you will often hear in this part of the world.

France briefly regained possession of New Orleans, but in 1803 US President Thomas Jefferson paid Napoleon $15 million for the entire Louisiana Territory. After that, Americans began boating down the river to New Orleans, which by then was quite famous not only for its parties but as a place where fast money could be made without too many questions asked.

The French Creoles, firmly entrenched in their town, did not exactly welcome the

Americans with open arms. As a result the Americans settled just upriver from the French Quarter on former plantations which had been sectioned off. A broad strip of land separated the French Quarter from the American Sector, and early on it was intended that a drainage canal be built on it. The canal was never built, however, and because frequent fights broke out between the French and the Americans the strip of land became known as the 'neutral ground' between the two sectors. New Orleanians to this day refer to the strip of land along the centre of a boulevard as the neutral ground. In every other American city it is known as a median. The original strip is now Canal Street, a broad, tree-lined boulevard which forms the now peaceful boundary between Uptown and Downtown.

THE CITY LAYOUT

New Orleans lies on a crescent-shaped land mass, carved out long ages ago by the mighty Mississippi, which provides yet another nickname: the Crescent City. The meanderings of the serpentine river wreak havoc with ordinary north, south, east and west directions. New Orleanians refer instead to 'lakeside' (toward Lake Pontchartrain), 'riverside' (toward the Mississippi), Uptown or upriver, and Downtown or downriver. The French Quarter and everything else below Canal Street is Downtown; above Canal Street is Uptown.

The French Quarter

Also called the Vieux Carré (Old Square), the French Quarter is the original colony founded by the French Creoles. Laid out in a perfect grid by French engineers in 1721, it's an easily walkable 96-square-block area bordered by Canal Street, Esplanade Avenue, Rampart Street, and the Mississippi River. The Quarter is a living museum, with about 7,000 residents and a host of hotels, guesthouses, restaurants, museums, jazz joints, quaint shops, expensive antique stores, and sleek shopping malls.

Narrow streets are lined with charming two-

and three-storey buildings of old brick, wood, and stucco, with gables and sloping grey roofs pierced with dormer windows. Many are painted with pastel colours, and all are adorned with fanciful architectural frostings. Filigreed ironwork, graceful galleries, broad fanlights, colourful shutters, and frilly gingerbread trim decorate houses and buildings not only in the Quarter but throughout the city. The Creoles built their houses flush with the sidewalk (often called *banquettes* here), and broad carriageways sweep from the street to hidden courtyards with lavish plants and graceful, tiered fountains.

The Greater New Orleans Bridge, over the Mississippi. Its cantilever span is one of the longest in the US

The heartbeat of the Quarter is Jackson Square, a pretty green park surrounded by a flagstone pedestrian mall. Serene, white St Louis Cathedral rises over an earthy scene of dixieland bands, tap-dancers, break-dancers, mimes, fire-eaters, clowns, banjo and bongo players, portrait painters, curious tourists, nonchalant locals going about their business, and a colourful cast of French Quarter characters.

A great place to get an overview of Jackson Square is on the promenade of Washington Artillery Park on Decatur Street. From there you have a splendid view of the Square, St Louis Cathedral flanked by the Cabildo and the Presbytere, and the twin Pontalba Apartments which line St Peter and St Ann Streets. On the other side of you is the

The Central Business District's offices and luxury hotels give meaning to the 'new' in New Orleans

Mississippi River. A close-up look at the river can be obtained by crossing the Riverfront Streetcar tracks and going over to Moon Walk, a wooden boardwalk which promenades right along the water. Over to the right you can see the high rises of the 'CBD'.

Central Business District
Formerly a sugar plantation where the Americans first settled, the CBD, as it is always called, is precisely what the name suggests: the centre of the city's business. This is the nerve centre for the 15-mile (24km) long Port of New Orleans, and the buildings house foreign agencies, government buildings, smart hotels, massage parlours, fast-food chains, department stores, the colossal Superdome, monuments, convention centres, and a host of other facilities.

At the foot of Canal Street, riverboats dock at
Spanish Plaza; and at the Canal Street Wharf
you can board the free ferry for a breezy ride
across to Algiers, an old residential district on
the West Bank. You can get a great view of
the city's skyline from the river, and the
round-trip ferry ride takes just half an hour.
At Canal and Carondelet Streets in the CBD,
you can board the St Charles Streetcar to
rumble and clang up St Charles Avenue and
see the Garden District and Uptown sights.

The Garden District and Uptown
As more immigrants poured in during the 19th
century, the city grew upriver, following the
curve of the Mississippi. Irish and German
immigrants settled in an area between
Magazine Street and the river, a

*Intricate decoration
and ironwork are
part of the
architectural
heritage which has
lately been treated
to careful renovation*

neighbourhood still called the Irish Channel, although the residents are now predominantly blacks and Cubans. This is not a good place for tourists to wander around.

St Charles Avenue, one of the city's loveliest streets, is the main thoroughfare through the Garden District and Uptown. The Lower Garden District, just past Lee Circle, is run down, but there are once-grand mansions now being renovated. The streetcar rolls beneath arching oaks, and as you approach Jackson Avenue, the lower boundary of the Garden District, magnificent homes and splendid gardens come into view. The Americans who built their Greek Revival, Italianate, and Queen Anne mansions in this area thumbed their noses at the Creoles' secluded courtyards by surrounding their

homes with beautifully landscaped gardens. The Garden District lies on the old Livaudais Plantation, which was at one time flooded, and the soil is rich with nutrients that produced the gorgeous vegetation in this aptly-named district. Sixth Street is a good place to jump off the streetcar and stroll around for a view of the elegant area. Upriver of the Garden District are the campuses of Tulane and Loyola Universities, across the Avenue from lush Audubon Park, with its wonderful Zoo.

Mid-City and Lake Pontchartrain

Mid-City is an old section of town which lies between the French Quarter and Lake Pontchartrain, cutting a wide swathe between New Orleans proper and St Tammany Parish on the North Shore. The Lake, a favourite playground of New Orleanians, is 40 miles (64km) long and 25 miles (40km) wide. The 25-mile (40km) long Lake Pontchartrain Causeway that crosses it is the longest in the world.

City Park, a luxuriant 1,500-acre urban oasis, is in Mid-City, as are the Fair Grounds, the main stomping ground of the Jazz and Heritage Festival and home of one of the city's two race tracks.

Greater Metropolitan Area

The Greater New Orleans Metropolitan area is comprised of St Bernard, St Tammany, Jefferson, and Orleans Parish, in which sits New Orleans proper. Louisiana is the only state in the US which calls its counties 'parishes', a hangover from the early Catholic colonial period. Metairie is a very old suburb to the west, covering acres and acres of former sugar plantations. The city sprawls over about 360 sq miles (930 sq km), 200 of which are more or less dry land. There are many waterways in these parts. The city lies about 5ft (1½m) below sea level, and has more canals than Venice, though they are not as conspicuous, and you don't have to get around by gondola or *vaporetto*. The population of the four parishes is 1,200,000 altogether, with about 600,000 people living in New Orleans proper.

WHAT TO SEE

◆◆
CEMETERIES

Because New Orleans lies well below sea level, 'burials' are in above-ground tombs. Many of the tombs look for all the world like tiny houses in a silent suburb, and for that reason the cemeteries are called Cities of the Dead. Almost all tombs are garnished with wrought-iron filigree. In the mid-19th century, J N B dePouilly, a graduate of the École des Beaux Arts, arrived here from Paris with illustrations of the French capital's Père Lachaise cemetery, and designed not only fine houses but final resting places as well. The oldest cemetery is **St Louis**

One of the three St Louis Cemeteries, where high water levels led to above-ground interment

Cemetery. The cemetery is near a crime-ridden area and you should not visit it alone. Go on a tour conducted by the Jean Lafitte National Park Service, 916-918 N Peters St, French Market (tel. 589-2636).

Churches and Monuments
◆
ANDREW JACKSON STATUE
Jackson Square
Right in the centre of a pretty green park, this colossal equestrian statue honours the hero of the 1815 Battle of New Orleans, fought downriver in the fields of Chalmette. The statue was erected in the 1850s, at which time the square

WHAT TO SEE

was named after General Jackson. Each year on 8 January, the anniversary of the battle, British, French, and American dignitaries gather for solemn ceremonies in nearby St Louis Cathedral and at the foot of the statue. From the very beginning, this square has been a centre of activity. It was Place d'Armes (parade ground) for the early French Creole colonists, who worshipped in St Louis Cathedral, shopped at the French Market, and gathered for social activities in the Square, which is situated in the French Quarter.

◆
CHURCH OF IMMACULATE CONCEPTION
130 Baronne Street, CBD
This Jesuit Church is a dramatic Moorish structure with twin onion-domed towers and horseshoe arches. Dating from 1930, the church is an exact replica of the original 1851 church on this site and much of the interior is from the

first church. The bronze altar, cast in Lyons, won first prize in the Paris Exposition of 1867-68. The statue of the Virgin Mary was to have been put in the royal chapel at Tuileries, a plan foiled when the French royals were forced to flee during the Revolution of 1848. The New Orleans congregation bought the statue in France for $5,000.

◆
FOREIGN PLAZAS
CBD
Sprinkled around the CBD, near the river, there are four foreign plazas paying tribute to countries which have figured prominently in the city's history. **Piazza d'Italia** (Poydras St) appeared in the opening scenes of the film *The Big Easy*. The monument that honours the Italians has a fountain built in the shape of

The award-winning Piazza d'Italia is a tribute to one of the many nations which have contributed to the city's history

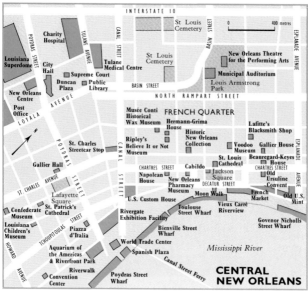

Map labels: INTERSTATE 10, Charity Hospital, St Louis Cemetery, BASIN STREET, New Orleans Theatre for the Performing Arts, Louisiana Superdome, City Hall, Tulane Medical Centre, St Louis Cemetery, Municipal Auditorium, Supreme Court, Duncan Plaza, Public Library, Louis Armstrong Park, New Orleans Centre, Post Office, NORTH RAMPART STREET, Musée Conti Historical Wax Museum, FRENCH QUARTER, Hermann-Grima House, Lafitte's Blacksmith Shop, Ripley's Believe It or Not Museum, Historic New Orleans Collection, Voodoo Museum, Gallier House Museum, St. Charles Streetcar Stop, St. Louis Cathedral, Beauregard-Keyes House, Gallier Hall, CHARTRES STREET, Cabildo, Old Ursuline Convent, Napoleon House, New Orleans Pharmacy Museum, Jackson Square, DECATUR STREET, Lafayette Square, Confederate Museum, St. Patrick's Cathedral, U.S. Custom House, Moon Walk, Vieux Carré Riverview, French Market, Old U.S. Mint, Louisiana Children's Museum, Piazza d'Italia, Rivergate Exhibition Facility, Toulouse Street Wharf, Govenor Nicholls Street Wharf, Aquarium of the Americas & Riverfront Park, Bienville Street Wharf, World Trade Center, Spanish Plaza, Mississippi River, Riverwalk, Convention Center, Poydras Street Wharf, Canal Street Ferry, CENTRAL NEW ORLEANS, 0 400 metres

Italy, and is the focal point of the annual Columbus Day celebrations. **British Place**, between the Hilton Hotel and the World Trade Center, is a circle of green grass with a rather unflattering statue of Winston Churchill. **Place de France**, between the WTC and the Rivergate, has a small but dazzling gold-plated statue of Joan of Arc. **Spanish Plaza** is a broad expanse of mosaic tile and a glorious fountain surrounded by tiles depicting Spanish coats of arms. This plaza is a centre of much activity, leading as it does to Riverwalk and riverboat landings. This is the venue for Lundi Gras, the big public masked ball which is held the night before Fat Tuesday (Mardi Gras).

◆◆◆
GALLIER HALL
545 St Charles Avenue
One of the finest Greek Revival structures still on its feet in the city, this building was designed in 1845 by James Gallier, Sr, who also had a hand in designing St Patrick's Cathedral, across Lafayette Square. Gallier Hall is a stately building with handsome Ionic columns and a pediment bearing sculpted figures of a blind Justice, Liberty (wearing a Phrygian cap), and Commerce (laden with symbols). In the mid-19th century, as a result of squabbling between the Creoles and newcomers, the city was divided into three municipalities. This area was the centre of government and

WHAT TO SEE

St Louis Cathedral dates back to the 18th century; two older buildings were destroyed by fire

social life for the second municipality. Gallier Hall, St Patrick's Cathedral, and Lafayette Square were the American Sector's equivalent of the Cabildo, St Louis Cathedral, and Jackson Square.
Open: Monday to Friday 09.00 – 17.00.
St Charles Streetcar.

◆
LEE CIRCLE
Robert E Lee, the South's great Civil War general, is immortalised in a statue that soars high above the traffic circle between the CBD and the Lower Garden District. This is one of the few places in town where you can get a sense of north, south, east, and west directions. The general, mounted on a 60ft (18m) column and floodlit at night, stares towards the north.
St Charles Streetcar.

◆
LOUISIANA SUPERDOME
1500 Poydras Street
The largest indoor facility of its kind, the home of the New Orleans Saints football team covers a total of 52 acres, with the Dome alone measuring 680ft (210m) in diameter. Tulane University's home games are played here, as well as the Sugar Bowl Classic. This was the site of the 1988 Republican National Convention. Guided tours are conducted daily, except during games and other

events (tel. 587 3808).
CBD Shuttle.
Open: 09.00-16.00 daily.

◆
OUR LADY OF GUADALUPE CHURCH
411 N Rampart Street
A charming little church dedicated in 1827. Its earliest function was as a mortuary chapel for victims of yellow fever and cholera, many of whom are buried in St Louis Cemetery No 1, right behind the church. The church houses yet another of New Orleans' legends, St Expedite. According to the oft-told tale, a crate marked *Expedite* was delivered to the church and inside the crate was a statue. Church employees expeditiously mounted the icon, which you can see just to the right when you enter the church. St Expedite is a rather militant looking chap who, like all other saints, is exhorted to 'Pray for us.' No one seems to know whom the statue represents. At midnight each Saturday night, this church celebrates a Jazz Mass, which is a beautiful blend of the city's religious and musical traditions. Situated on the fringe of the French Quarter.

◆
PONTALBA APARTMENTS
Jackson Square
Twin three-storey row houses lining St Peter and St Ann Streets; 16 on each street. Built in 1849 and 1851, the Pontalbas are among the oldest apartment houses in America. They were financed by the Baroness Micaela Almonester

de Pontalba, another of the Crescent City's legendary characters. Her father, Don Andres Almonester y Roxas, was a wealthy Spanish merchant, who donated funds for the restoration of St Louis Cathedral and the Cabildo after the 1788 fire. She married Celestin Pontalba, and lived in France until the Revolution of 1848, at which time she returned to New Orleans. She and her father-in-law, the baron, were not excessively fond of each other – to the extent that one night he shot her. Thinking he had killed her, he then shot himself. He died; she survived. The Baroness's family initials 'A' and 'P' are worked into the intricate cast-iron grillwork on the buildings' façades. The apartments were built in the European style, with shops on the first floor and apartments above them. The apartments are among the most coveted in the city (though not the most expensive). Naturally you can pop into the shops, but not into the private apartments – except for the 1850 House, which is worth seeing. Situated in the French Quarter.

◆◆◆
ST LOUIS CATHEDRAL
Jackson Square
The Cathedral of St Louis King of France soars like a hymn over the playground of musicians and mimes in its front yard. This is America's oldest active Roman Catholic cathedral. The first church on this site was a small wooden structure built in 1727 and

destroyed by the fire of 1788. The present church dates from the 1790s, and was remodelled in the 1850s to the specifications of French architect J N B dePouilly. Named after Louis IX of France, the cathedral is the seat of the archdiocese of New Orleans. Though modest in comparison to the great cathedrals of Europe, the church has lovely ceiling frescos and stained-glass windows. The windows in the front of the church were donated by the Spanish government. The cathedral is in the French Quarter. Visitors welcome between church services.
Open: Monday to Saturday, 09.00-17.00; Sunday 13.00-17.00.

♦
ST PATRICK'S CATHEDRAL
724 Camp Street
This church, patterned after York Minster in England, was built in the late 1830s as a house of worship for Irish Catholics.
St Charles Streetcar.

Houses and Mansions
♦
BEAUREGARD-KEYES HOUSE
1113 Chartres Street
Built in 1826, this handsome Greek Revival raised cottage was for a brief period the home of Confederate General Pierre Gustav Toutant Beauregard, the man who ordered the first shot fired at Fort Sumter (that was the shot which began the War Between the States).
In 1944, the house was bought by novelist Frances Parkinson Keyes, who restored the slave quarters and used them as a studio. Furnished with lovely period antiques, the house is shown by costumed guides. A pretty English Garden is adjacent to the house.
Open: Monday to Saturday 10.00-15.00.

♦♦
BROWN HOUSE
4717 St Charles Avenue
Henry Hobson Richardson, a Louisiana native and one of America's foremost 19th-century architects, developed a distinctive style that became known as Richardsonian Romanesque. A superb example of the style can be seen in the W P Brown house, a rough-textured stone mansion with exotic Syrian arches, deeply recessed windows, and broad arcades. The largest, and most costly, mansion on the Avenue is surrounded by elegantly manicured lawns. A private residence. Uptown. St Charles Streetcar.

♦♦
COLONEL SHORT'S VILLA
1448 Fourth St, Garden District
A huge Italianate mansion, designed in 1859 by noted architect Henry Howard, who also designed Nottoway and Madewood plantations. A cast iron fence in a motif of cornstalk and morning glories surrounds the mansion and its lovely landscaped gardens. A private residence; visitors are not allowed in. St Charles Streetcar.

The past preserved in Gallier House

◆◆
DOULLET HOUSES
400 and 503 Egania Street
Also called the 'Steamboat Houses', these identical twins were built in 1905 by steamboat captain Milton Paul Doullet for himself and his son. Looking exactly like frilly riverboats, the houses have three decks, exterior double stairs dropped like gangplanks from the second tier, pilothouses topside, and huge wooden beads, graduated in size, strung like great necklaces between slender posts. The pilothouses have a distinctly Oriental motif; the captain is said to have been greatly influenced by a Japanese pavilion he saw at the St Louis-Louisiana Purchase Exposition in 1903. Fantastic houses. It is a shame you can't see the interiors, but they are private homes. Located in Bywater downriver from the French Quarter. Take a cab.

◆◆◆
GALLIER HOUSE
1118-32 Royal Street
Architect James Gallier, Jr, famous son of a famous father, built this house for himself in 1857. It's one of the best researched and most carefully restored of the museum houses. Although the Galliers were not French (they came here from Ireland), they adapted to Creole life, and this house is an outstanding example of how the well-heeled Creole lived. A fascinating house with lovely

WHAT TO SEE

Longue Vue House and Gardens

period furnishings and a gorgeous formal parlour. As part of the tour, videos are shown in which the techniques of *faux marbre* and *faux bois* are described and demonstrated. Gallier House is in the French Quarter.
Open: Monday to Saturday, 10.00 -16.30.

◆◆
HERMANN-GRIMA HOUSE
820 St Louis Street
An American-style townhouse, dating from 1831, this house is particularly interesting for the detached kitchens, where Creole cooking demonstrations take place on Thursdays during the winter. The house itself is a lovely mansion, and the curator arranges special

exhibits from time to time; for example, during a recent Hallowe'en he had the house done up in 19th-century Creole funereal trappings. The former stable is a gift shop. Situated in the French Quarter.
Open: Monday to Saturday 10.00-15.30.

◆◆
JOHNSON HOUSE
2343 Prytania Street
Now the exclusive Louise S McGehee School for Girls, this Second Empire beauty was built in 1872 as a townhouse for wealthy sugar planter Bradish Johnson. It was designed by New Orleans architect James Freret, who studied at the

Ecole des Beaux Arts in Paris. Garden District. St Charles Streetcar.

♦♦♦
LONGUE VUE HOUSE AND GARDENS
Bamboo Road
Once the estate of a New Orleans cotton broker and his wife, heiress to the Sears fortune, the house is styled after the great country estates of England. The mansion is furnished with the original English and American antiques, French and Oriental carpets, and a collection of Wedgwood and Leeds creamware. Walls are hung with antique wallpaper and Chinese rice paper. There are changing exhibits in the galleries. The house is surrounded by eight acres of landscaped gardens, such as the Portuguese Canal Gardens and the Spanish Court, modelled after the 14th-century Generalife Gardens of the Alhambra. Concerts and elegant galas occasionally take place here, as well as daily tours. The best way to reach

the house is by taxi.
Open: Tuesday to Saturday, 10.00-16.30;
Sunday, 13.00-17.00 (last tour 16.15).

♦♦
MUSSON HOUSE
1331 Third Street
Decorated with filigreed galleries, this Italianate house was built in 1853 for Michel Musson. The New Orleans Postmaster was an uncle of French Impressionist painter Edgar Degas, who was sometimes a guest in the house. A private home. Garden District. St Charles Streetcar.

♦
PITOT HOUSE
1440 Moss Street
A perfect example of the West Indies-style homes built by the early planters. The house was built in 1799, and in 1810 it was bought by New Orleans Mayor James Pitot as a country home, hence the name (which is pronounced *pee*-toh). It is furnished with 18th- and 19th-century Louisiana and American antiques.

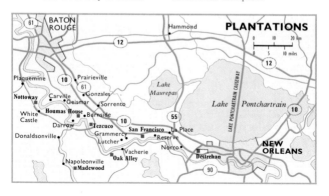

Esplanade bus.
Open: Wednesday to
Saturday, 10.00-15.00.

◆◆
ROBINSON HOUSE
*1415 Third Street, Garden
District*
One of the largest and loveliest
houses in the Garden District,
this house was built right after
the Civil War (1865) for Walter
Robinson, a Virginian. The first
and second storeys are exactly
the same height, and another
unusual feature is the curved
portico. This house is believed
to have been the first in New
Orleans to have indoor
plumbing. A private
residence, so you will have to
admire it from outside the
fence.
St Charles Streetcar.

◆
TOBY'S CORNER
*2340 Prytania Street, Garden
District*
This rather simple (but not
small) raised cottage is
believed to be the oldest
house in the Garden District,
built in about 1838 for a
Philadelphia businessman
named Thomas Toby.
Surrounded by a fence and
luxuriant trees, the house is
raised well above the ground
on brick pilings. A private
residence.
St Charles Streetcar.

◆◆
WEDDING CAKE HOUSE
5809 St Charles Avenue
This elaborate confection is a
Colonial-Greek Revival
masterpiece with wrap-around
upper gallery, handsome

cornices, dormers and
numerous Ionic columns. It was
concocted in the late 19th
century. A private residence;
no admission.
St Charles Streetcar.

Mississippi Plantations
◆◆◆
PLANTATION HOMES
The Great River Road laces
along the Mississippi River
from New Orleans to Baton
Rouge. 'Progress' has
destroyed much of the beauty
of the drive, but several of the
old plantation homes have
been beautifully restored and
are open for tours. All of the
antique-filled mansions are on
the National Register of
Historic Places. Several have
been sets for movies, and
some of them are sumptuous
(and pricey) bed-and-
breakfasts. The nearest
(though not the most
handsome) is an hour's drive
west of the city. If you would
rather not make the drive
yourself, there are several
companies conducting guided
tours to the area. Among them
are the well-known Gray Line
(tel. 525-0138) and Tours by
Isabelle (tel. 367-3963), the
latter offering minivan tours.
Some of the highlights are:
Houmas House, a splendid
Greek Revival mansion which
was the set for *Hush, Hush
Sweet Charlotte*, starring Bette
Davis and Olivia De Havilland.
The house is surrounded on
three sides by massive
columns, and a carriageway
connects the main house to an
earlier cottage. Guides clad in
antebellum gowns will show

The trees after which Oak Alley plantation was named predate the 1839 house by a century

you, among other things, the magnificent spiral staircase.
Madewood, another Greek Revival masterpiece, is one of the most charming of the old plantations. It, too, is a movie star, as well as a luxurious bed and breakfast. Included in the overnight price are wine and cheeses in the parlour, followed by a gourmet candlelit dinner in the elegant formal dining room. Expect plenty of old-fashioned pampering.
Nottoway, the South's largest plantation, is a palatial Greek Revival-Italianate mansion surrounded by 22 columns and set in glorious grounds. The White Ballroom, with its original chandeliers and magnificent Corinthian columns, is famed in this part of the country. This is also a B&B.
Oak Alley, setting for the Don Johnson and Cybil Shepherd TV remake of *The Long Hot Summer*, is a white-columned mansion famous for the spectacular alley of 28 arching live oaks in the grounds.
San Francisco, a 'Steamboat Gothic' house which does, indeed, look like a frilly riverboat run aground, is noted for its ornate millwork and ceiling frescos.

Museums
◆◆◆
CABILDO
Jackson Square
Flanking St Louis Cathedral, the Cabildo is a lovely 18th-century building with mansard roof and dormer windows. It is

WHAT TO SEE

the second cabildo (Spanish governing council) on this site, the first one having been destroyed in the fire which gutted the colony 1788. This building has held the government offices of France, Spain, the Confederate States of America, and the United States. Transfer papers for the 1803 Louisiana Purchase were signed on the second floor of the building, and when the Marquis de Lafayette visited New Orleans in 1825 this is where he stayed. Now part of the Louisiana State Museum complex, the Cabildo has several exhibition halls with displays including Napoleon's death mask. In 1988, 200 years after the fire that destroyed the first building, fire damaged much of the roof and ceiling. Virtually all of the important historical documents (and the death mask) were saved, and restoration of the building has been underway recently. French Quarter.
Open: Wednesday to Sunday, 10.00-17.00.

◆
CONFEDERATE MUSEUM
929 Camp Street
Memorabilia pertaining to the War of Northern Aggression, as the Civil War is sometimes more or less jokingly called in this neck of the woods. Historical documents, paintings, some personal effects of Confederate President Jefferson Davis, blood-stained flags, uniforms, and part of General Robert E Lee's campaign silver service. St Charles Streetcar.

Open: Monday to Saturday, 10.00-16.00.

◆◆
HISTORIC NEW ORLEANS COLLECTION
533 Royal Street
The archives of this museum contain the original blueprints for every historic building in New Orleans. The house itself, a former private home, is built around a lovely central courtyard and has a fascinating history. It dates from 1792, and survived the fire of 1794. The Williams Gallery on the first floor has changing exhibits about the city's history, and for a small fee a guide will give you a tour of the house and tell you all about it.
Open: Tuesday to Saturday, 10.00-16.30.

◆◆
1850 HOUSE
525 St Ann St, Jackson Square
A restored, three-storey apartment in the 'lower' (downriver) Pontalba Apartments gives you a taste of how well-to-do Creoles lived in the mid-19th century. Furnished with period antiques. Handsome canopied beds, antique dolls, interesting old-fashioned kitchen. Visitors tour it on their own. Situated in the French Quarter.
Open: Wednesday to Sunday, 10.00-15.00.

◆◆◆
LOUISIANA CHILDREN'S MUSEUM
428 Julia Street
A delightful place for the youngsters, filled with fun and

educational hands-on exhibits. Children can float inside a bubble; 'broadcast' news in the Kids Eyewitness Newscenter; buy groceries in a supermarket; operate a crane to load and unload cargo in the Big City Port. Take a taxi.
Open: Tuesday to Sunday, 09.30-16.30.

◆◆
LOUISIANA NATURE AND SCIENCE CENTER
11000 Lake Forest Boulevard
An 86-acre wildlife preserve offering a tempting in-town taste of the surrounding swamps and bayous. There

Confederate Museum flies the flag

are nature trails, hands-on exhibits for children, a planetarium and lots of special events. The Center organises backpacking trips, moonlight hikes, and a variety of outdoor activities. Take a taxi. There are planetarium shows Tuesdays to Fridays at 16.00, and on weekends at noon, 14.00 and 16.00.
Open: Tuesday to Friday, 09.00-17.00; Saturday and Sunday noon-17.00.

◆◆
MUSÉE CONTI HISTORICAL WAX MUSEUM
917 Conti Street
Very well executed tableaux depict various events in the city's history, ranging all the way from 1682, when La Salle

Louisiana Historical Association's
CONFEDERATE MUSEUM
OPEN MONDAY - SATURDAY
10:00AM-4:00 PM
BY ADMISSION

WHAT TO SEE

followed the Mississippi down to its mouth, to the 1987 wax figure of former Governor Edwin Edwards. All of the beloved legends are represented: Jean Lafitte, Andrew Jackson, Marie Laveau, Napoleon, Madame LaLaurie – the works. The wax figures are lavishly costumed, the faces startlingly life-like, and the captions quite accurate. French Quarter.
Open: daily 10.00-17.30.

◆◆
NEW ORLEANS MUSEUM OF ART
City Park
Pretty white neo-classic building in lush subtropical surroundings. The permanent collection includes paintings, sculptures, drawings, and prints that examine the development of Western Civilisation from the pre-Christian era to the present. Prominently featured are the works of French Impressionist Edgar Degas, who had relatives in the city and visited here occasionally, and of Peter Carl Fabergé, master jeweller to the Czars of Russia. The Fabergé exhibit includes the Basket of Lilies of the Valley, created in 1896 for Empress Alexandra. The Treasures of King Tut and the Search for Alexander are among the special exhibits that have been presented to the public at the museum.
Admission to the museum is free all day Thursday. Esplanade bus.
Open: Tuesday to Sunday, 10.00-17.00.

◆
PHARMACY MUSEUM
514 Chartres Street
This wonderful, musty old place was the shop of Louis J Dufilho, Jr, America's first licensed pharmacist. There is a fascinating collection of ancient tools of the trade, including voodoo powders and *gris-gris* potions. Lots of ancient prescriptions, apothecary jars, and such. Also a great black-and-rose

Confederate troops were imprisoned in the US Mint during the Civil War

Italian marble soda fountain dating from 1855. French Quarter.
Open: Tuesday to Sunday, 10.00-17.00.

◆
PRESBYTERE
Jackson Square
Almost identical to the Cabildo, which is on the other side of St Louis Cathedral, the Presbytere was built in the late 18th century to house the priests who served the cathedral. It houses changing exhibits and, like the Cabildo,

is part of the Louisiana State Museum complex. A bizarre-looking Confederate submarine snoozes in the arcade of the building, hardly the vehicle by which the South will rise again. Guided tours of the French Quarter regularly start from here.
Open: Wednesday to Sunday, 10.00-17.00.

◆
RIPLEY'S BELIEVE IT OR NOT
501 Bourbon Street
Even if you are not excited by two-headed animals, shrunken heads, and the world's tiniest or tallest this or that from Robert Ripley's Odditorium, you might drop in to see the fabulous feathered costumes of the Mardi Gras Indians. A Mardi Gras tradition dating back to the 19th century, the 'Indians' are actually blacks who parade in tribes on Fat Tuesday. French Quarter.
Open: daily, 10.00-midnight.

◆◆
US MINT
400 Esplanade
Built in 1835, this was the first major branch of the United States Mint. It went out of the money-making business in 1861 when the Civil War broke out. Now a part of the Louisiana State Museum, the building houses exhibits about two of the city's best known traditions. The Mardi Gras exhibit has a collection of shimmering sceptres, crowns, and costumes. In the Jazz Exhibit, there are musical instruments that belonged to famous jazzmen (including Louis Armstrong), and various

memorabilia. Well-documented panels trace the history of jazz. Behind the Mint, in mint condition, there is a restored streetcar from the old Desire line which inspired Tennessee Williams to write *A Streetcar Named Desire*. French Quarter.
Open: Wednesday to Friday, 10.00-17.00.

◆
VOODOO MUSEUM
724 Dumaine Street
This dimly-lit little hole in the wall is the place to find out all about Marie Laveau, New Orleans' own Voodoo Queen. There are displays of various voodoo accoutrements, such as potions, dolls, *gris-gris* charms and anything else you would need to do your voodoo. In a back room there is a voodoo altar. The museum conducts voodoo tours, including an all-day jaunt into the swamps to visit haunted plantations. French Quarter.
Open: Sunday to Thursday, 10.00-19.00 (till 22.00 Friday and Saturday).

Parks
◆
AQUARIUM OF THE AMERICAS AND RIVERFRONT PARK
Ground was broken in 1987 for this new $40 million attraction, which is expected to be fully operational by early 1991. It covers 16 acres, including a huge aquarium that holds a million gallons of water and 4,000 different species of sea creatures. The nine-acre landscaped park surrounding the aquarium is under

A 'Greek temple' adds unusual decoration to Audubon Park

construction at the time of writing. The aquarium is on the Mississippi River between the Canal Street Wharf and the Jackson Brewery.

◆◆
AUDUBON PARK
6500 St Charles Avenue
A wonderful 400-acre urban oasis designed by Frederick Law Olmsted, who also designed New York's Central Park. A mere pocket-park compared to the Big Apple's vast playground, the Big Easy's version is nonetheless splendidly adorned with grand old live oak trees, palms, lagoons, and lush tropical plants. Two hundred years ago

this was the Foucher plantation where, in 1795, Etienne de Bore figured out how to granulate sugar for commercial purposes, thereby revolutionizing the sugar industry. In 1884-85, the World's Industrial and Cotton Centennial Exposition was on this site. At that time the world's largest building, covering 31 acres, stood on what is now an 18-hole golf course. In addition to the golf links, there is a jogging track, a stable, tennis courts, and delightful places for picnicking or doing absolutely nothing. The wonderful Audubon Zoo occupies the back portion of the park.
The Park is closed to all except bikers and pedestrians. St Charles Streetcar.

◆
CHALMETTE BATTLEFIELD
Chalmette, LA (6 miles/9.6km downriver from the city)
This is the site of the famed Battle of New Orleans, fought in 1815 between British and American forces. The British, under the command of Major General Sir Edward Pakenham, massed to attack and take New Orleans, but were defeated by Major General Andrew Jackson and a motley crew of Tennessee Volunteers and pirates donated by Jean Lafitte. This was the last battle of the last war ever fought between Great Britain and the United States. In fact there is not a lot to see at Chalmette. However, aficionados of military history may enjoy strolling over the green fields and imagining the bloody struggle. The Chalmette Cemetery was established in 1864, and is, for the most part, the final resting place of Union soldiers who were killed in this area during the Civil War. Chalmette is operated by the Jean Lafitte National Historical Park, and in the Visitors' Center Park Rangers give talks four times daily about the battleground. They also provide a self-guided walking and driving tour brochure that points out all of the batteries and ramparts and fully describes the battle. The Beauregard House is a lovely plantation house (open but unfurnished) and there are picnic grounds in the park. You can drive there from Canal Street by heading for North Rampart Street, which

merges first with St Claude
Avenue and then with LA
Highway 46, which passes the
park; or you can cruise down
on the *M/V Voyager* or the
Creole Queen, both of which
make excursions that allow you
time to hear a lecture and
stroll about.
Open: 09.00-17.00 every day
(tel. 589-2636).

♦♦♦
CITY PARK
*northern end of Esplanade
Avenue*
One of the nation's most
naturally lavish urban parks,
City Park's 1,500 acres are
dressed with majestic live
oaks, the likes of which you
may never have seen. Several
of them are over 800 years old,
with tattered grey shawls of
Spanish moss and massive
boughs bent over to touch the
earth. There are 8 miles (13km)
of man-made lagoons lacing
through the park, where you
can fish or row out among the
swans, and beautifully
landscaped Botanical Gardens
replete with fountains and
statuary. The *P G T
Beauregard* is a vintage
miniature train that runs along
a 2½-mile (4km) scenic route.
Star attraction of the
amusement park is The Last
Carousel, dating from the
1890s, where you can ride
antique flying horses, but there
are also antique car rides and
a ferris wheel. Children's
Storyland is a theme park with
Mother Goose characters,
puppet shows, and story-telling
hours. At the Casino, you can
rent bikes and boats, get a

*Man-made lagoons attract many
species of waterbird to City Park*

permit for fishing in the
lagoons, or simply take time
out for a bite to eat. There are
four lush golf courses, with pro
shop, golf carts, and clubhouse
restaurant, plus a double-deck
100-tee driving range. There is
also a 39-court tennis centre,
and the park is awash with
baseball and softball
diamonds.
Esplanade bus.

Landmarks
♦
CONGO SQUARE
Louis Armstrong Park
Many jazz historians believe
that this was the birthplace of
jazz. In the 18th and 19th
centuries, slaves congregated
here each Sunday afternoon to
chant, sing, and dance to the
rhythm of 'tam-tams' and

'bones'. The Afro-Caribbean rhythms are most certainly heard in jazz music. While the music is a blend of many sounds, there is one man believed to have been the first person to play what is now called jazz. Buddy Bolden was a black cornet player who is said to have been able to listen to a tune, memorise it instrument by instrument, and then improvise on it. Congo Square was going strong when Buddy was a boy, and he probably took the rhythmic beats he heard there, mixed them with a myriad of other sounds, and created his own music from the secrets in his soul. Congo Square, which is in front of Municipal Auditorium, is now officially named Beauregard Square but most locals still call it by its original name.

◆
CORNSTALK FENCE
915 Royal Street
One of only two such fences in New Orleans (the other being around Colonel Short's Villa in the Garden District), the cast-iron fence has a design of morning glories intertwined with ears of corn. Cast in a Philadelphia foundry, the intricate fence arrived by ship in New Orleans, and was erected in 1834. French Quarter.

◆
COURT OF TWO LIONS
710 Toulouse Street
Atop tall stone walls, two stone lions face each other across a broad wooden gate. Behind the gate, the house, which dates from the early 1800s, is now a shop and the courtyard is filled with statues, softly gurgling fountains, and other garden accessories made by local craftsmen. French Quarter.

◆◆
CUSTOMS HOUSE
423 Canal Street
The huge grey granite building that occupies the entire 400 block of Canal Street was begun in 1848, but the War Between the States caused a delay in construction and it was not completed until 1881. During the war the partially completed building was headquarters for General Benjamin 'Spoons' Butler (derisively called 'Spoons' by Southerners because the Yankee general stole sterling silver flatware from New Orleans homes during Union

WHAT TO SEE

occupation of the city). The building was also a federal prison during the war, at one point housing 2,000 Confederate soldiers. Although there's nothing very exciting about the façade, this building contains one of America's finest examples of Greek revival architecture. The Great Marble Hall, where general customs business is transacted, is a marvel of white marble. Measuring 95ft (29m) by 125ft (38m), the 54ft (16m) high room boasts 14 Corinthian columns, each 41ft (12.5m) high and 4ft (1.2m) in diameter, cut from white Italian marble that was shipped to this country in blocks. Stone-cutters in Boston fashioned the pillars, bases, and capitals, which were then brought by ship to New Orleans. On the river side of the hall is a large marble bas-relief depicting the Great Seal of the State of Louisiana, flanked by Jean Baptiste Bienville, who founded the city in 1717, and General Andrew Jackson, who defended it in 1815. A stunning room. CBD. Open: weekdays 09.00-16.30.

◆
FARMERS MARKET
French Market
For more than 160 years farmers have been bringing their produce to sell in the long open sheds strung out behind the French Market. Bins are piled high with fruits and vegetables, and the narrow aisle is almost always crowded with locals and tourists. Craftsmen, too, display their wares, and on weekends

Gruesome tales of cruelty and torture surround the Haunted House

there's a flea market that spills out into the surrounding area. French Quarter.

◆
FIRST SKYSCRAPER
640 Royal Street
Built in about 1795, this weathered masonry house has a curved wall that follows the contours of the rooms. It was built for Dr Yves LaMonnier, whose third-floor study is an architectural masterpiece. The house originally had three floors, and the top floor is said to have been added so that the house could retain its 'tallest' title. The house is also known as 'Sieur George, after a character in a short story by 19th-century New Orleans writer George Washington Cable. French Quarter.

◆
HAUNTED HOUSE
1140 Royal Street
Hair-raising tales are told about Madame Delphine LaLaurie, yet another of the city's legends. She occupied this house in the early 1830s, and became famous for her fabulous soirées. She was also the subject of much gossip regarding the condition of her servants, who appeared terrified and emaciated. On one occasion she was seen beating a small black slave girl, for which offence she was hauled into court, fined, and released. On 10 April, 1834, a fire broke out in the house. Attempting to save the contents, neighbours broke into an upper room, where they came upon a scene of incredible horror. Seven servants, whose broken bodies were chained in neck and leg irons, screamed and moaned in the smoke-filled room. The next day a newspaper account of the tragedy accused Madame LaLaurie of starting the fire, and an angry mob gathered outside the house. The LaLauries leapt into a carriage and beat a hasty retreat, at which point the mob stormed the house and sacked it. Delphine died some years later in Europe, and her body was secretly brought back to New Orleans for burial. It is said that the house to this day is haunted by shrieks, screams and moans. It's a private residence now, and you could not go in even if you wanted to. French Quarter.

◆◆◆
LABRANCHE BUILDINGS
700 block of Royal St and 600 block of St Peter Street
The most photographed corner in the city is St Peter and Royal, where lacy ironwork drapes the galleries of the LaBranche Buildings. The eleven separate three-storey brick row houses that make up the complex date from about 1840.

◆◆
MADAME JOHN'S LEGACY
632 Dumaine Street
George Washington Cable wrote many tales about New Orleans Creoles. Madame John was a fictional character in his story *'Tite Poulette*, and this house was her legacy. Cable beautifully describes the house in the story. This is a West Indies-style house at the

Over 150 years old, the St Charles Streetcar rattles through town

centre of a hot local debate. The argument is among historians, and at issue is whether this house or the Old Ursuline Convent is the oldest intact structure in the Lower Mississippi Valley (holding the title of 'oldest' is dear to the hearts of Southerners). Some contend that the house which was originally built in 1726 was destroyed by the fire of 1788; others maintain that it was only partially damaged and that additions were made after 1788.

The house is now a part of the Louisiana State Museum and is only occasionally open. It has recently been closed for restoration (tel. 568-6968). French Quarter.

◆◆
MARDI GRAS FOUNTAINS
Lakeshore Drive
Just outside City Park, across Marconi Drive, the circular fountains spout 60ft (18m) cascades, brilliantly lit at night in the Mardi Gras colours of gold, green and purple. They do this, at least, when they are working; before setting out to see them check with the tourist centre to see if the fountains are flowing. Not far from the parking area, ceramic tiles are emblazoned with the names, emblems and colours of the various Carnival krewes. Mid-City. Take a cab.

◆◆
OLD URSULINE CONVENT
1114 Chartres Street
Madame John's Legacy
notwithstanding, this building is
the only undisputed survivor of
the fire and a fine example of
classic French Colonial
architecture. It is the second
building on this site, the first
having been built in 1727. The
present building dates from
about 1745, and housed the
Sisters of Ursula who arrived in
New Orleans in 1727 and
moved into this convent in
1749. This building housed the
first convent in Louisiana; the
first Catholic school; the first
Indian school; the first black
school; and the first
orphanage. It now holds
archives of the New Orleans
archdiocese. Visitors are not
allowed to enter. French
Quarter.

◆◆◆
PIRATE'S ALLEY
*between Jackson Square and
Royal Street*
Pirate's Alley and its twin,
Père Antoine's Alley, sneak
alongside St Louis Cathedral
and the Cathedral Gardens
behind the church. The
flagstone passageway was cut
in the 1830s, long after Jean
Lafitte and his band of
Baratarians had vanished.
However, the theory persists in
legend-loving New Orleans
that the pirate and General
Andrew Jackson met here to
plan the strategy for the Battle
of New Orleans. It never
happened, but the atmosphere
here is nonetheless quite
exotic. In an apartment at 624

Pirate's Alley, Nobel prize
winner William Faulkner wrote
his first novel, *A Soldier's Pay*.

◆
RIVERGATE EXHIBITION CENTER
foot of Canal Street
Once the city's primary
convention centre, its duties
now usurped by the mammoth
Convention Center nearby, the
Rivergate is home to the Food
Fest held in July and hosts
trade shows and exhibits. On
the Sunday night before Mardi
Gras, the entire Bacchus
parade, floats and all, rolls into
the Rivergate. CBD.

◆◆◆
ST CHARLES STREETCAR
The Crescent City's rumbling,
movable museum is the
world's oldest continuously
operating street railway
system. It began service on 26
September, 1835, and in the
early days steam locomotives
from England pulled the cars.
The city used to be laced with
streetcar lines, including the
Desire line that inspired
Tennessee Williams to write *A
Streetcar Named Desire*. For
many years, the St Charles
Streetcar was the only one
operating, but in 1988 the
Riverfront Streetcar began
breezing along the Mississippi.
A National Historic Landmark,
the St Charles Streetcar is for
many Uptown New Orleanians
merely a convenient way of
getting to work in the CBD. For
many others, including locals
as well as tourists, this is a
terrific way to clang along to
the Garden District, Audubon
Park and the Zoo, Tulane and

Loyola Universities, Riverbend, the Camellia Grill, and all the other Uptown places. You can get a general view of Uptown by boarding the Streetcar at Canal and Carondelet in the CBD and riding all the way to the end of the line at Palmer Park. There you can pay another 60 cents and take a seat on the opposite side to see the sights on the other side of the street. A round trip covers just over 13 miles (21km) and takes about an hour and a half.

STORYVILLE

Not a trace remains of New Orleans' notorious red-light district, which is not to say that it isn't still much discussed. Photographs of Storyville girls were the basis for the Brooke Shields film *Pretty Baby*. This is another of the city's cherished legends, and the legend is well-grounded in fact. In 1744, a French officer complained that there were not ten women of blameless character to be found in the entire city. After more than 150 years of half-hearted attempts to control prostitution, city alderman Sidney Story introduced legislation that restricted women who were 'notoriously abandoned to lewdness' to a 12-block area. That area, between Iberville, Basin, North Robertson, and St Louis Streets, came to be known as Storyville, after the author of the ordinance. The stories about Storyville are colourful. Luxurious 'sporting houses', like Lulu White's Mahogany Hall and the palace of Josie Arlington, were famed

Louisiana's old 'roads': the bayous

far and wide. A Blue Book, listing the various houses, the girls, and the girls' 'specialities' was published. The more prosperous of the pleasure palaces hired musicians to entertain in the parlour, and many an early jazz great worked in the red-light district. (No one knows exactly how the word 'jazz' came to be used, but it *is* known that 'jass' was a terribly dirty word bandied about in the infamous houses). Storyville flourished for 50 years until it was closed down in 1917 on orders of the US Government. Most of the buildings were razed in the 1930s to make way for the high-crime federal housing project that now occupies the site. Don't wander around in the area looking for landmarks. There are none, and the area is not safe. Only the memory remains.

◆
WILDLIFE & FISHERIES BUILDING
400 block of Royal Street
You may wonder about the big white marble building which occupies the entire block across the street from Brennan's. It was built in 1907 as the Civil Courts Building and later housed offices of the Wildlife & Fisheries agency. The empty building is used for occasional galas, such as a recent Hallowe'en when banners proclaimed it *Castle Dracula* for a spectacular masked ball. Debates continue to rage in Louisiana about legalising casino gambling; this

is the building most often discussed as a possible casino. French Quarter.

◆◆
WORLD TRADE CENTER
2 Canal Street
The streamlined skyscraper houses import/export offices, foreign agencies, and so forth. But you can get a superb view for miles around on the 31st floor. A glass elevator eases up the outside of the building to Viewpoint, an observation deck, where enlarged, captioned photographs fill you in on what can be seen in the distance. There are also telescopes in case you want a closer look. A great place to get your bearings.
Open: every day 09.00-17.00. CBD.

Swamps and Bayous
South Louisiana is laced with waterways, ranging from the Mississippi River to the 800,000-acre Atchafalaya Basin to the brackish bottle-green bayous that snake through the state. (*Bayou* is an Indian word meaning stream). Once upon a time the bayous were the highways and byways of Chocktaw and Chitimacha Indians. Pirates hid out in the murky reaches of the swamplands, and when voodoo was outlawed in New Orleans, Marie Laveau led her cultists into the bayous, where they continued to practise their mysterious rites. These days the swamps and bayous are of more interest to botanists, birdwatchers, hunters, and fishermen – though of course, there are those tales of an

awesome swamp monster stalking about in the Honey Islands Swamp. (See also **Peace and Quiet**, below.) There are several tours to give you a taste of bayous and swamps in fairly close proximity to the city. Each of the tours listed below offers a different type of outing to the visitor.

Annie Miller Terrebonne Swamp & Marsh Tours (tel. 879-3934).

Louisiana has an alligator population of about 500,000, and most of them slither about in the bayous and swamps of South Louisiana. Annie Miller is known in the area as 'the lady who talks to 'gators'. Her boats cruise out into the bayous, habitat of her friend, Smilin' Sam, the alligator. Her tours depart from Houma, a town 57 miles (92km) south of New Orleans on Highway 90.

Honey Island Swamp Tours (tel. 242-5877 or 1-641-1769). Dr Paul Wagner is a wetland ecologist who knows the secluded sloughs and waterways of Honey Island Swamp like the back of his hand. Honey Island Swamp is one of the nation's least altered wetlands, alive with alligators, herons, egrets, wild boars, and, perhaps, a swamp monster. Dr Wagner's flatboat tours are both fun and informative. When you call for reservations you can arrange for round trip transportation between your hotel and the departure point.

Tours by Isabelle (tel. 367-3963).

A Cajun Bayou Tour is a five-hour trip that includes a narrated history of the Cajuns and a boat tour through bayous and cypress swamps, hosted by a Cajun alligator hunter and fur-trapper who knows all about the bayous and its denizens. Tour price includes the hotel pick-up and return service.

◆◆◆
AUDUBON ZOO
6500 Magazine Street
The Zoo, one of America's five best, occupies 58 acres of lush Audubon Park. More than 1,000 animals, including a white tiger, amble about loose in landscaped areas resembling their home turf. Wooden walkways ramble through an African savannah, replete with rhinos and hippos; the Louisiana Swamp Exhibit, where alligators laze on the banks of a bayou; an Australian outback with emus and kangaroos; and much more. You could spend days here.

The Mombasa mini-train travels through the back part of the Zoo. The elephant and camel rides in Wisner Children's Village are enormously popular. Near the River, Monkey Hill was constructed in the 1930s so that the children of these flatlands would know what was meant by the word 'hill'.

Magazine St bus or St Charles Streetcar.

Open: Monday to Friday, 09.30-17.30; Saturday and Sunday 09.30-18.00; closes one hour later during the summer months.

PEACE AND QUIET

Wildlife and Countryside in and around New Orleans

Lying at the mouth of the Mississippi, New Orleans is an ideal base from which to explore the marshes, bayous and swamps of the coastal plain of the deep south of America. This coastal strip is extensive, stretching up to 30 miles (48km) inland where alluvial soils from the river's delta have been deposited; but inland, forested hills and valleys add to the richness of the countryside surrounding the city. New Orleans' position

Herring gull – cities such as New Orleans provide rich hunting grounds for this ubiquitous bird

on the coast of the Gulf of Mexico also means that visitors can explore and enjoy remote and exotic beaches.

The resident flora and fauna of the swamps and marshes of southern Louisiana and Mississippi are varied and fascinating and comprise everything from epiphytic plants such as bromeliads to colourful frogs, alligators and elegant herons. During spring and autumn migration, hundreds of thousands of migrant birds also pass through the region and in winter it is one of America's most important wildfowl locations. Fortunately, the best times of year to observe wildlife also coincide with the most acceptable weather, the summers being hot and humid.

City Surroundings
The city is surrounded by water and so, not surprisingly, the wildlife reflects the freshwater and marine environments. To the south of the city, the Mississippi winds its way towards the sea while to the north lies Lake Pontchartrain, which opens through Chandleur Sound into the Gulf of Mexico.
From the southern shores of Lake Pontchartrain, large numbers of wintering wildfowl, gulls and terns can be seen. Many of these birds can also be viewed at close range on the lagoons and ponds in New Orleans' City Park, whose northern boundary is close to the shore of the lake. American coots mingle with ring-necked ducks and the occasional goldeneye on the lagoons and close to the lake shore, while Forster's, Caspian and royal terns plunge into the deeper water in search of fish. Four species of gull are regularly present in New Orleans in the winter months with occasional rare visitors to add to the list. In bird books, they seem easy to identify, shown in clean, bright illustrations. In practice, however, it can be a real challenge, because even an

individual gull's plumage varies according to age and time of year.

The beaches of the Gulf of Mexico make ideal nesting grounds for birds such as this Sandwich tern

The largest species in the area is the herring gull, a familiar bird on both sides of the Atlantic. Its pale grey back is a similar shade to the smaller ring-billed gull, but the latter's

banded bill, menacing eye and grey-green (not pink) legs distinguish it. Laughing gulls are smaller and have neat, black hoods in summer which fade to an irregular pattern of dirty marks in winter. Smallest of all is the diminutive Bonaparte's gull whose pale, almost translucent underwings are a good clue to its identity. A short drive on the far side of Lake Pontchartrain along Interstate routes 10 and 59 leads to the Pearl River Wildlife Management Area, where wetland wildlife can be viewed from the road and from a swamp nature trail. Red-shouldered hawks and Mississippi and swallow-tailed kites circle overhead, while anhingas dive in search of fish. Alligators remain a constant threat to the water birds and green and Louisiana herons and snowy egrets keep a wary eye open. In the safety of the trees, red-bellied, hairy, downy and pileated woodpeckers probe the timber for nest holes and wood-boring grubs.

The Gulf of Mexico and the Offshore Islands

The Mississippi delta and the Gulf of Mexico beyond are home to vast numbers of birds. Many of these stop off on migration while others spend the winter feeding in the mosaic of marshes, pools and islands. On the more remote islands and shell beaches the visitor can see birds which are found nowhere else on the mainland, some of which are truly oceanic species.

PEACE AND QUIET

From the land, much of the shore is inaccessible by car or foot and special boats have to be arranged. However, you can sometimes glimpse the wildlife spectacle from boat trips and from some of the coastal roads, especially around Gulfport in Mississippi. The road to the town of Venice, southeast of New Orleans at the mouth of the Mississippi, provides a view towards the Delta National Wildlife Refuge, home to thousands of snow geese and other wildfowl in winter. Fortunately, however, two islands, both within a day's journey from New Orleans, can be reached by car and are well worth a visit. Grand Isle lies almost due south of the city and is reached after a tortuous journey along US route 90 and provincial route 308. However, the drive itself provides excellent views of egrets, herons and wildfowl. When you eventually reach the beaches, mudflats and mangroves of Grand Isle, little blue herons, ibises, willets, pelicans and other birds are easily seen.

In the spring, nesting terns, including sandwich and little, race through the skies, sometimes joined by black skimmers; but without a doubt, the masters of the air are the magnificent frigatebirds which frequent the island throughout the summer. With an immense wingspan of nearly 8ft (2½m), these aerial pirates attack other seabirds, forcing them to regurgitate their last meal. Deer Island, south of Biloxi in the state of Mississippi, is easily reached from New Orleans by driving east along the coastal US route 90. Although privately owned, access is open to the public and boats often leave Biloxi. The island can be superb during a massive influx of migrants in spring, but has a wealth of breeding and wintering species. Waders, such as willets, and rails and terns frequent the marshes and beaches, while woodlands hold, among others, warblers, woodpeckers and great crested flycatchers.

Open Water

The immense Mississippi and the coastal lakes surrounding New Orleans harbour vast numbers of resident birds which are supplemented in the winter by wildfowl from all across North America escaping to the mild climate around the Gulf of Mexico. The numbers of birds reflect the abundance of aquatic life found beneath the surface of the water – including alligators, turtles and large numbers of fish, some of which live nowhere else in the world. Fish life is abundant in the Mississippi and adjoining rivers and lakes. Streamlined garpike, a favourite food of alligators, are common and found eastward throughout the southern US. In contrast, the paddlefish, a curious relative of the sturgeon, is found only in the waters of the Mississippi and its tributaries, the fish getting its name from the curious paddle-like extension above its mouth. It uses this projection to stir up mud on the river bed and the animals that this disturbs are eaten.

In almost every pond, lake and river backwater you are likely to find turtles and terrapins. Snapping turtles, mud turtles, box turtles and terrapins are

Snapping turtles can be every bit as unfriendly as they look

all common and are interesting subjects to watch from the water's edge. Some species like to bask in the heat of the sun and many are beautifully marked. The snapping turtles, however, could in no way be described as elegant. Capable of giving humans a powerful and painful bite if handled carelessly, this fierce predator will tackle fish, frogs and even

small birds, which it grabs by surprise and drags underwater. It is deceptively strong and is very flexible, and preferably should not be handled at all.

Above the surface of the water, the fish and smaller turtles have other enemies.

Many species of heron and egret stalk the shallows, while terns plunge-dive and anhingas swim gracefully through the water. While some of the wildfowl residents and winter visitors, such as mergansers and buffleheads, are fish eaters, others eat blue-winged teal can be seen on open water, taking to the wing in a sudden fright if alarmed.

Freshwater swamps

As the Mississippi river winds its way south between the boundaries of Louisiana and Mississippi states, it creates extensive marshes and swamp woodlands of cypress, cottonwood, pecan and live oak. These wetlands are a haven for numerous fish, frogs and toads, many of which fall victim to alligators which still lurk in quiet corners. Wildfowl are abundant in the winter and numerous egrets and herons are present throughout the year, supported by the abundant freshwater life.

The warm weather and constant humidity means that, for many plants, obtaining enough water to survive is not a problem. As a consequence, many grow not in the soil but, instead, on the branches and trunks of the swamp trees. The roots of these 'epiphytic' plants serve to anchor the plant firmly to the tree and moisture is collected from the air and as it runs down the bark. Ferns and orchids grow in profusion as do bromeliads, the well-known 'air-plants', with spiky leaves and red flower spikes.

Birdlife in the swamps is fascinating and varied. Purple gallinules, for example, are a wonderfully colourful mixture of purple, green and blue. The precise colour of the gallinule varies according to the level of light, since the feathers have a sheen, but they always set off

In flight, black vultures have an air of menacing grandeur, but on the ground they just look ungainly

aquatic vegetation and many others filter out small animals from the muddy sediments. Large flocks of mallard, pintail, shoveler, green-winged and

PEACE AND QUIET

the red, yellow and blue beak and frontal shield, and the bright yellow legs.

Pure white snowy egrets vie with little blue herons in terms of elegance. As if to complement the egret's smart plumage, it has jet-black legs and distinctive yellow feet and shins. Its larger relative, the great egret, also wades cautiously through these swamps, with its long plumes dragging in the water. Because they generally remain motionless, waiting for a fish or frog to swim into range, American bitterns are difficult to see. Their mottled brown plumage gives them a good camouflage among the tangled vegetation that they prefer to haunt. The same is true of their tiny relative, the least bittern. Since it is such a small bird, the least bittern is able to walk

Ferns and lichens are among the most common 'epiphytic' plants in Mississippi's wetlands

through the vegetation without making it collapse, and when sure of itself will sometimes reward the observer by venturing into the open.

The Coastal Marshes

From the shores of Louisiana, coastal marshes stretch inland for up to 30 miles (48km) and comprise a mosaic of pools, lakes, bayous and swamps. The waters of the Gulf of Mexico are held back from these marshes by the sandy beaches behind which they form. However, the sea still exerts an influence on the swamplands, and for a considerable way inland, the water is brackish.

Because of the lush feeding to be had on both sides of the beaches, vast numbers of waders and wildfowl spend the winter in this wetland sanctuary, protected by its inaccessibility. Many birds also breed close to the shore, Forster's terns preferring the beaches, while black-necked stilts and rails choose the safety of the rushes and reeds that make up the marshland vegetation.

Semi-palmated plovers, short-billed dowitchers, semi-palmated sandpipers and willets feed along the shoreline and occasionally in the landward marshes and pools, especially at high tide. Willets, so named because of their call, are rather nondescript, grey waders when at rest. However, as soon as they take to the air, their unmistakable black and white marked wings make them easy to identify.

Here and there throughout the coastal marshes, well-vegetated pockets of land rise above the uniformly level wetland. These islands are similar in many ways to the tropical 'hammocks' found in Florida's Everglades and comprise hardwood species of trees with cypresses around their swampy margins.

While the swamps hold the fish, frogs and vegetation which provide food for the birds, these wooded outcrops of dry land are a refuge and sanctuary in which many of them nest. Great-blue, little-blue, green and Louisiana herons all have scattered colonies throughout the marshes often in the company of snowy and great egrets and roseate spoonbills.

Black-crowned and yellow-crowned night herons both leave their roosts to feed at dusk just as the other diurnal herons and egrets are returning. The foliage of the trees contains a variety of insects which, in turn, feed migrant warblers and orioles. Noisy groups of resident boat-tailed grackles often take to the wing, while overhead both Mississippi and swallow-tailed kites can occasionally be seen.

The Mississippi

The mighty Mississippi river, known to the North American Indians as the 'father of waters', dominates the states of Louisiana and Mississippi. It also provides a convenient geographical divide between the east and west of the continent since its 2,350-mile

PEACE AND QUIET

(3,780km) long course takes it from its source in Lake Itaska in Minnesota, within a few miles of the Canadian border, to the Gulf of Mexico. The meanderings of the Mississippi through Louisiana, as it approaches the sea, have created a wide, flat alluvial valley. The rich soil in these lands of marshes, ox-bow lakes and bayous, known as bottomlands, once supported extensive woods of oak, cypress and willow, festooned with lichens and Spanish moss. Although much of the land adjoining the river has come under the influence of man, the stretch of the river between Baton Rouge and St Francisville in West Feliciana is still well worth exploring. From the banks of the river, gulls, Forster's terns and occasional brown pelicans can be seen close to New Orleans but as you travel upriver, ducks, grebes, herons and egrets become more frequent. Black vultures are frequently seen along the banks as they scavenge for dead remains, looking deceptively small when on the ground. In the air, however, they soon reveal their mastery of the skies and remain aloft seemingly without effort, the white panels on their otherwise black wings being a sure pointer to recognition. During the autumn and winter the Mississippi becomes immensely important to vast numbers of wildfowl and other water birds from northern America. The lower reaches are in the flight path of hundreds of thousands of wildfowl which include mallard, American wigeon, ring-necked and ruddy ducks, as well as grebes and terns, which all converge from September onwards. Many remain throughout the winter, enjoying the mild climate and rich supply of food.

On the Wing

Each spring, countless millions of birds begin their long migration from central and South America back to their breeding grounds in North America and Canada. By August and September these are deserted again and the adult birds and their young start the return journey. Winters in the northern latitudes are harsh and the warmth and abundant insect life in the tropics and sub-tropics more than make up for the energy exerted migrating. Many of the migrant birds are tiny, most warblers being only 4 or 5 inches (12cm) long, which makes the journey seem even more remarkable. In spring, most begin the journey by flying straight across the Gulf of Mexico from the northern coast of South America, heading for the Gulf coast of Louisiana and Mississippi.

In spring, the weather in New Orleans is generally warm and settled. When these favourable conditions prevail, migrant birds fly straight in off the sea and rapidly disperse inland, leaving little evidence that migration has taken place. However, if a cold front sweeps down from the north

As its name suggests, the yellow crowned night heron sets out on its fishing expeditions after the sun has set

bringing cold, rainy weather, things are altogether different. Exhausted birds desperately make for the first land they sight and phenomenal numbers of birds literally drop in on the coast and are collectively known as a 'fall'. If these rather precise weather conditions occur between the middle of March and the middle of May, more than 15 species of warbler, such as chestnut-sided warblers, flycatchers, vireos and many other passerines may be found side by side. Anywhere along the coast can be good but Deer Island, off Biloxi and Grand Isle, south of New Orleans are renowned spots. In the autumn, the birds migrate in the reverse direction and adverse weather conditions do not produce the dramatic 'falls' of spring. But, tropical storms and hurricanes blow tired migrants off course, and again the coastal areas should be searched.

PEACE AND QUIET

The coasts and marshes around New Orleans are good for waders in autumn, some species of which winter in the region while others pass through on their way to South America. Lesser yellowlegs, semi-palmated and western sandpipers are all commonly seen, while more unusual species like pectoral and white-rumped sandpipers occur regularly among the mixed flocks.

Farmland and Open Country
As you drive inland from New Orleans, a lot of the rolling countryside of Louisiana, which once was covered by forests, has been cleared and where the soil is rich enough, small-holdings and agriculture have taken over. Much of the farming is small-scale, with orchards and small fields being a familiar sight and, especially in areas where the agriculture has been abandoned, the rough fields and scrubby borders provide a haven for insect life and birds.

Rough, grassy areas are much favoured by butterflies. Elegant monarchs, red admirals and sulphurs dance from flower to flower and swallowtails such as the pipe-vine swallowtail even visit garden flowers in rural areas. North American sparrows and buntings also find plenty of food in the form of seeds and insects, and the vegetation provides them with cover. Chipping sparrows, who earn their name from their chipping, trill-like song, make their nests

Pipe-vine swallowtail butterflies are often seen in grassy areas

among bushes.

Owing to their habit of creeping through the vegetation rather than flying when disturbed, American sparrows can be difficult to see. Dickcissels, eastern meadowlarks and colourful

characteristic wing-flicking flight action. They share the air with barn swallows who, as their name suggests, make their nests in houses and out-buildings.

As you drive along the quiet back roads, mockingbirds and catbirds flash in front of the car, the latter recognisable by their uniformly grey plumage with brick-red feathers under the tail. Roadside fences and overhead wires provide ideal perches for eastern kingbirds and loggerhead shrikes, alert, predatory birds which tackle large insects relative to their small size.

After dark, some of the more shy, nocturnal animals of the region come out of hiding and are occasionally caught in car headlights. Skunks, racoons, armadillos and white-tailed deer may flash through the lights and unfortunately some are transfixed and become road casualties.

Woodlands and Forests

Along the winding valley of the Mississippi and its tributaries, and inland from the coastal marshes, extensive forests once cloaked the states of Louisiana and Mississippi. Generations of farmers and plantation owners have cleared much of the woodland but there are still tranquil areas of forest within a day's drive from New Orleans.

The woodlands of the river valleys differ markedly from the pine forests found on the hills and uplands north of New Orleans. The dominant trees beside the rivers are

indigo and painted buntings, on the other hand, sometimes perch on bushes and fence posts, making them much easier to see.

The mournful cooing call of the mourning dove, from which its name derives, is a familiar sound and parties of two or three are often seen flying swift and low with

PEACE AND QUIET

hardwoods with pecan, sweetgum and swamp red oak growing in drier areas while cypress and tupelo prefer their roots in water. Frogs, terrapins and alligators haunt the swamp pools while in the branches of the trees, lizards scurry among the epiphytic lichens and orchids. Woodpeckers are common in these swamp forests with five species commonly seen. The large size and loud call of the pileated woodpecker make it difficult to overlook, and flickers and red-bellied, downy and hairy woodpeckers also occur. Overhead, red-shouldered hawks and Mississippi kites circle above their nests in the tree tops. North of New Orleans and Lake Pontchartrain lie the Florida Parishes, a region of rolling hills which support forests of slash and longleaf pines. A speciality of these wooded areas is the red-cockaded woodpecker, a species which drills its nest hole into a living tree. The subsequent trickle of resin down the trunk is a good clue to the hole's occupancy and sometimes attracts feeding butterflies. Elsewhere in the woodland, fritillaries, wood nymphs and swallowtail butterflies seek flowers as sources of sugar-rich nectar. Blue jays, brown-headed nuthatches and numerous warblers feed among the leaves and branches, and nearer the ground, red-eyed vireos search for insects among the fallen pine needles and branches. Small parties of

bobwhite quails scurry along and grassy clearings can hold several species of North American sparrow.

Racoons and armadillos also occur in the woodland but their largely nocturnal habits mean they are only likely to be seen at dusk. Grey squirrels are more easy to see and are one of the most successful of North

Grey squirrel – undeniably pretty, but not always popular

America's mammals, being widespread in the US and introduced to many other parts of the world.

National Wildlife Refuges

Although a long drive from New Orleans, the swamps south of Lake Charles in the west of Louisiana are well worth a visit. Extensive marshes lie within the boundaries of Lacassine and Sabine National Wildlife Refuges and provide a spectacle throughout the year with wildfowl in winter and nesting birds in summer. While much of the area is totally inaccessible, abundant wildlife can be seen from roads and the refuge authorities sometimes arrange boat trips at certain times of the year. The headquarters of Lacassine NWR, which contains over 30,000 acres of marsh, is approached from the town of

Lake Arthur, southwest of Lafayette. Within the swamps of sawgrass, small pockets of cypress trees grow and ryegrass and oats have been planted for the wintering wildfowl to graze. Sixteen thousand acres of man-made pools in the west of the refuge attract vast numbers of water birds.

During the autumn and winter, the Lacassine refuge itself is closed to the public, providing a peaceful sanctuary for snow and white-fronted geese, blue-winged teal, pintail, shoveler and ring-necked duck, and the largest concentration of fulvous tree ducks in the US. Although the best areas cannot be visited, a great deal can still be seen from the approach road and around the headquarters. During the summer, when the refuge is open to the public, alligators, otters, nutria, skunk and mink haunt the pools and anhingas, egrets, herons, purple gallinules and white ibises all breed here.

Further west, the Sabine NWR can be reached on State route 27 which heads south from Interstate 10. This road eventually leads to the Gulf of Mexico at Holly Beach but its route, which runs through the refuge, encounters freshwater marsh and brackish swamps near the coast, and almost every species for which the refuge is famous can be seen on this route.

Alligators are abundant and mink, otter and armadillo can also be found. Thousands of ducks, including mallard and green-winged teal feed alongside roseate spoonbills, herons and egrets. Snow and white-fronted geese, for which the refuge is also famous, mainly frequent the western and eastern fringes bordering Lakes Sabine and Calcasieu, but flocks can turn up anywhere.

Manatees

The coastal waters of the Gulf of Mexico are home to one of the most bizarre mammals found in North America. The manatee or sea cow is a docile animal which spends its whole life in water grazing on submerged vegetation and, despite its rather inelegant appearance, it is thought to have given rise to stories of mermaids. Although seriously threatened by disturbance and pollution, it still lives in the waters off New Orleans. Manatees reach an immense size and commonly exceed 10ft (3m) in length and a weight of 1,100lbs (500kg). With their bristly lips, they grab mouthfuls of water plants, much of which they eat while submerged, since they can remain underwater for up to half an hour.

Small groups of up to half a dozen are sometimes encountered in the brackish waters of river mouths along the Gulf coast as they cruise slowly along. Generally the water which they inhabit is murky and so often it is only the head which is visible. However, sometimes their paddle-like tail-flipper is seen when they dive.

FOOD AND DRINK

Virtually everything in New Orleans centres around food. When New Orleanians are not actually eating they are usually discussing their last meal, the best chef, the newest restaurant, and so on. There is good reason for the focus on food. It is difficult to find really bad food here, although you will rarely hear that from the locals. New Orleanians have notoriously fussy palates. New Orleans is the birthplace of Creole cuisine; the cradle of Cajun food is to the west of the city. Creole cuisine originated in the city and is exemplified by rich sauces. The French Creole cuisine evolved over a couple of centuries, perhaps beginning when the early French settlers began to add some of the local herbs and heady spices to traditional French recipes. This region abounds with exotic produce and is rich with sea creatures. Later arrivals – African slaves, Spaniards, Irish, Italians, Yugoslavs, and Greeks – all added a pinch of this and a pinch of that, and the pot thickened.

Cajun food, created in the bayous of south Louisiana, may bring a tear or two to your eye. Often called the country cousin to Creole cuisine, Cajun food is more robust and tends to be on the fiery side.

You will find terms here that will be unfamiliar to you, even if you have dined in a Creole or Cajun restaurant. New Orleans waiters are accustomed to translating

Seafood figures prominently in the New Orleans diet

menu items for visitors, but here are some of the ubiquitous terms and dishes:

Andouille (*ahn*-doo-ye): spicy Cajun sausage.

Bananas Foster: famed New Orleans dessert, concocted of bananas sautéed in butter, cinnamon and sugar, flambéed in brandy, and served over vanilla ice cream.

Barbecue shrimp: not a traditional barbecue at all. Large shrimps are cooked in their shells, with heads, legs and tails intact, and served in a butter and garlic sauce. You peel them and eat them.

Beignet (*bin*-yea): square, hole-less doughnuts liberally sprinkled with powdered sugar.

Boudin (*boo*-dan): hot, spicy pork mixed with onions, cooked rice, herbs, and stuffed in sausage casing.

Chicory (*chick*-ory): a herb, the roots of which are ground, roasted, and used to flavour the potent coffee New Orleanians favour.

Courtbouillon (coor-boo-*yon*): a rich, spicy stew of fish fillets, tomatoes, onions, and sometimes mixed vegetables.

Crawfish (sometimes spelled crayfish but always pronounced crawfish): these little crustaceans, which resemble toy lobsters, turn up on many a south Louisiana table. Often called 'mudbugs' because they flourish in the mud of fresh-water streams, they come simply boiled or in etouffees or bisques.

'Dressed': when you order a sandwich you will be asked if you want it 'dressed,' which means with mayonnaise, lettuce, and tomato.

Good food is a frequent topic of conversation in the 'Big Easy'

FOOD AND DRINK

Etouffee (*ay*-to-fay): a succulent tomato-based sauce with rice and shrimp or crawfish.

Grillades (*gree*-yads): squares of broiled beef or veal, often served with grits for breakfast.

Grits: coarsely ground hominy grain with a taste resembling corn. Served piping hot for breakfast.

Gumbo: a thick soup with almost endless variations but always involving rice.

Jambalaya (jum-bo-*lie*-yah): a many-splendoured thing involving rice, tomatoes, ham, shrimp, chicken, celery, onions, and lots of spices.

Muffuletta: a sandwich roughly the size and shape of a dinner plate, though much thicker, made with Italian meats and cheeses and loaded with garlicky olive salad. You can get whole, half, and quarter portions.

Pain Perdu (lost bread): French toast, but made here with loaves of French bread rather than slices of white bread.

Po-Boy: another sandwich extravaganza; sliced French bread filled with either fried oysters, shrimp, roast beef, ham, or whatever. Very popular here.

Pralines (*praw*-leen): made of sugar, water, and pecans, with lots of variations.

Red Beans and Rice: traditionally served on Monday in Creole homes, this is kidney beans cooked with rice, sausage, and seasonings. A hearty, very inexpensive dish.

According to legend, the world's first cocktail, the Sazerac, was concocted here in the 19th century by a Monsieur Peychaud. The original involved Sazerac brandy, bourbon, bitters and absinthe. The latter is now illegal in the US, and the cocktail has boiled down to bourbon and bitters in a glass, spun in the air to coat it with an absinthe substitute. Fascinating to watch, but not a drink for the faint of heart. The Hurricane that you see touted all over town originated at Pat O'Briens, which still makes the best one, from 4½ ounces (130g) of dark rum mixed with passionfruit and other juices. The Ramos gin fizz is gin, cream, egg whites, orange flower water, and soda. The mint julep of song and legend is an old-time drink of bourbon, mint and quinine – possibly the South's favourite drink.

Restaurants

There are hundreds of restaurants and countless bars and cafés in New Orleans. American restaurateurs use the terms 'restaurant' and 'café' rather loosely. A restaurant is never referred to as a café – unless the owner uses the term for reasons of his own – but a café is often called a restaurant. To confuse things further, there are often classy cafés and run-down restaurants. Some of the best seafood in the city is served in ramshackle joints on Lake Pontchartrain.

Fast-food chains are sprinkled all over town – McDonald's,

FOOD AND DRINK

Wendy's, and New Orleans' own Popeye's, which serves spicy fried chicken and plump buttermilk biscuits – a good choice if you're in a hurry. Coffee shops, cafeterias, and grills fall somewhere between the fast-food and restaurant categories; casual spots with few amenities and often open throughout the day.

As for bars, the city is full of those that serve only alcohol. However, there are also oyster bars where you stand at the counter and watch the oyster shuckers shucking while you eat. New Orleanians consume tons of oysters.

In general, lunch is served between noon and 14.30 or 15.00. Many places start serving dinner as early as 18.00 and the last order is taken at 21.30 or 22.00. Since the definitions are blurred, it isn't feasible to say that 'cafés' are usually open all day; however, there are several places where you can stop in throughout the day for a meal. There are a few 24-hour eateries, which are noted below.

The up-market restaurants require jackets for men, but not necessarily a tie. 'Proper attire' usually means no shorts or jeans.

During the summer you can walk in to even the most famous restaurants and be seated without a reservation. Such is not the case in the autumn and spring, certainly not during Mardi Gras. During busy seasons you will need to book weeks in advance for a table at one of the 'Big Five'

(Antoine's, Arnaud's, Brennan's, Commander's Palace, and Galatoire's).

Acme Oyster House, 724 Iberville St, French Quarter (tel. 523-8928). Very popular with locals. Stand-up marble counter for oysters and beer; tables in the back; sandwiches also served. Open every day.

Andrea's, 3100 19th St, Metairie (tel. 834-8583). Superb Northern Italian and continental cuisine, beautifully presented in a handsome restaurant. Fine display of antipasti. Fresh homemade pastas and pastries. Baby white veal, seafood, game, and beef dishes. Sunday brunches with live Italian music are fun. Not cheap. Open daily (closed for lunch Saturdays). Take a taxi.

Founded in 1840, Antoine's has created some legendary dishes

Antoine's, 713 St Louis St, French Quarter (tel. 581-4422). America's oldest family-run restaurant (established in 1840), where oysters Rockefeller and pompano en papillote were created. The French Creole restaurant is greatly favoured by old-line New Orleanians. Delectable souffléed (puff) potatoes; *filet mignon marchand de vin* is legendary. *À la carte* menu, all in French. Stroll around and look at the various rooms, especially the Rex Room, with its displays about the King of Carnival; the 25,000 bottle wine cellar; and the Mystery Room. Jackets required. Quite costly. Closed Sundays.

Arnaud's, 813 Bienville St, French Quarter (tel. 523-5433). Classic Creole cuisine in a lovely restaurant with leaded glass windows, mosaic tile floors, slowly revolving ceiling fans, lots of greenery. Another favourite of old-guard New Orleanians. Bananas Foster, flambéed at the table side, is superb. Sunday jazz brunches are great fun. The musicians make a big fuss of children, who love it. Arnaud's Grill, with a polished wood bar and player piano is a fine place for an afternoon or before-dinner drink. Upstairs a Mardi Gras room exhibits Carnival gowns worn by Germaine Wells, daughter of the founder. Lunch Monday to Friday; dinner every night; brunch Sundays. Expensive.

FOOD AND DRINK

Back to the Garden, 207 Dauphine St (tel. 524-6915). A simple little place serving health food specialities such as stir-fry vegetables, spinach salad, vegetarian quiche, and cheese enchiladas. Also on the menu are several sandwiches, all in a health food mode. Very inexpensive, and if you are staying in the Quarter they will deliver to your hotel. Open Monday to Saturday 09.00-16.00. French Quarter.

Bailey's, Fairmont Hotel, CBD (tel. 529-7111). Classy café with stained-glass canopy over the bar. Full menu, including breakfasts, sandwiches, lunches, complete dinners. Pleasant atmosphere which you will have plenty of time to enjoy while you wait to be served. Inexpensive to moderate. Open 24 hours a day.

Brennan's, 417 Royal St, French Quarter (tel. 525-9711). 'Breakfast at Brennan's' is famed the world over. Eggs Sardou, Eggs Houssard and Eggs Benedict are among the

classic dishes. Creole sauces and soups are marvellous. Guests dine in one of twelve elegant rooms, and there is a pretty courtyard bar where you will probably have to nurse a drink even if you have reservations. Service is sometimes quite hurried because of the overflowing crowds. Dinner is an equally smart affair, and attire more formal than for brunch.

Café du Monde, an ideal setting for beignet-eating and people-watching

Expensive. Open daily.

Café Maspero, 601 Decatur St, French Quarter (tel, 523-6250). Word leaked out a long time ago about the big, over-stuffed sandwiches and thick-cut french fries, and you may have to queue up with the locals to get in. Enormously popular and very casual. Open all day, often crowded. No music, but plenty of loud chatter. Open 11.00-23.00; Saturday closes at midnight. Inexpensive.

Café du Monde, 813 Decatur St and St Ann St, French Market (tel. 525-4544). An institution, operating on the same site for more than 100 years. The open-air café (there are tables inside as well) is the traditional last stop after a night on the town. The entire menu is printed on the paper napkin holders: beignets (three to an order); café au lait or ordinary coffee; milk; and freshly squeezed orange juice. A great people-watching spot, liked by locals as well as visitors. Never closes. Cheap.

Camellia Grill, 626 S Carrollton Ave (tel: 866-9573). A maître d' hôtel choreographs the crowds who flock here to sit at the counter (no tables) and feast on plate lunches, juicy hamburgers, waffles, homemade desserts (banana cream pie is delicious; so is pecan pie). Open daily 08.00; closes 01.00 Sunday to Wednesday, 02.00 Thursday to Saturday. Very inexpensive. Uptown, on Streetcar route.

Caribbean Room, Pontchartrain Hotel, 2031 St Charles Ave (tel. 524-0581). Seafood and steaks done in

FOOD AND DRINK

classic Creole style in a chic rose-hued room with gas chandeliers and a graceful fountain. Frequented by Uptowners and the celebrities who like to stay in the famous hotel. The dessert speciality is Mile-High-Pie, which is actually about 8 inches (20cm) in height and involves peppermint, chocolate and vanilla ice cream, meringue, and chocolate sauce. Classical music provides background for Sunday brunch. Open daily except for lunch on Saturdays. Expensive. Garden District, on Streetcar route.

Charlie's Steak House, 4510 Dryades (tel. 895-9705). More than 60 years ago this restaurant created the New Orleans style of broiling steaks in butter. No menu; the waitress just gives you a choice of steaks and names the side dishes: onion rings; salads; potatoes au gratin. A plain, simple place, the walls are decorated with photos of New Orleans Saints football players who love to tackle the huge steaks. Lunch and dinner Tuesday to Friday; dinner only Saturday; closed Sundays. Expensive. Take a taxi.

Chez Helene, 316 Chartres St and 1540 N Robertson, French Quarter (tel. 525-6130) and Mid-City (tel. 947-1206). Model for the TV series *Frank's Place*, this is the place for old-fashioned soul food. Cornbread, biscuits, fried chicken, blackeyed peas, red beans and rice. Very, very casual. Chef Austin Leslie is a local celebrity. Open daily 07.00; closes Sunday to Thursday 22.00; Friday and Saturday 23.00. Inexpensive.

Coffee Pot, 714 St Peter St, French Quarter (tel. 524-3500). An institution since 1898, but old-world charm was lost when

Courtyard luxury is a trademark of the Commander's Palace Restaurant

the place was renovated. Still a good place for plantation breakfast (ham, eggs, grits, wonderful biscuits), pain perdu, shrimp Creole, jambalaya, red beans and rice. Heavenly pecan pie (ask them to warm it and top with whipped cream). Local business people stop in a couple of times a day for coffee breaks. Open every day 08.00 till 01.00 or 02.00. Inexpensive.

Commander's Palace, 1403 Washington Ave (tel. 899-8221). Arguably the best restaurant in the city and a great local favourite. Charming Victorian house with lush courtyard. Preferred seating is in the Garden Room, but you almost have to know someone to get a table there. The food is superb, no matter where you are seated or what you order. Menu features French, Creole, and American dishes, and everything is fresh. The jazz brunch originated here, and it's a lot of fun, with balloons festooning the tables and a peripatetic trio. Open daily for lunch and dinner (jazz brunches Saturday and Sunday). Very expensive. Garden District. St Charles Streetcar.

D H Holmes Cafeteria, 220 Dauphine St, French Quarter (tel. 561-6141). Informal place, convenient for shoppers or sightseers in the CBD or Quarter. Generous servings of Creole dishes, seafood, salads, and homemade pastries. Open daily 07.00-19.00. Inexpensive.

Deanie's, 1713 Lake Ave (tel. 831-4141). Fried catfish, huge seafood platters, boiled crawfish. Very casual place for hard-core seafood devotees, of whom there are legions in New Orleans. Food comes in iron skillets and small cauldrons. Enormous portions. Open every day 11,00-22.00 or 23.00. Inexpensive. Bucktown; take a taxi.

Esmeralda's, 219 Dauphine St (tel. 529-5741). A little hole in the wall, where a full breakfast is about $2 and daily lunch specials include standards such as red beans and rice and jambalaya. Closed Sundays. Very inexpensive. French Quarter.

Flagon's A Wine Bar & Bistro, 3222 Magazine St (tel. 895-6471). This started out a few years ago as a chic wine bar, and has grown into a chic eatery as well. Very popular with locals, it features a caviar bar as well as nouvelle cuisine. Among the offerings are pasta carbonara and grilled shrimp with fettuccine and tasso. Dining is in Art Deco rooms, and there's a Sunday jazz brunch. It is informal, but you will need reservations, especially on weekends. Open for lunch and dinner. Expensive. Uptown.

Galatoire's, 209 Bourbon St, French Quarter (tel. 525-2021). Another French Creole restaurant with a loyal old-line clientele. The menu, several pages long, lists chicken, seafood and steaks. Crawfish etouffee is not on the menu, but it is there if you ask for it. Wonderful French bread. Stylish, mirrored room, usually noisy and crowded. The

FOOD AND DRINK

restaurant takes neither reservations nor credit cards. Everyone queues up to get in (even the late Duke and Duchess of Windsor when they dined here). Open from 11.30 until 21.00, and you can avoid long queues if you arrive for lunch around 13.30 or 14.00 and early for dinner. On Sunday afternoons Galatoire's is a veritable salon, with regulars table-hopping to greet one another. Jackets after 17.00 and all day Sunday. Closed Mondays. Moderate prices.

Golden China, 7136 Downman Rd, East New Orleans (tel. 241-8944). Friendly, family-run restaurant serving inexpensive Hunan, Cantonese, and a few Szechuan dishes. Very small, simple place; food portions are enormous. You get a lot for your money here. Has a loyal following of locals; take a taxi. Closed Sundays. Inexpensive.

Grill Room, Windsor Court Hotel, CBD (tel. 523-6000). Luxurious room with marbled floors, Austrian drapes, yet a casual atmosphere. Continental and American foods are featured: steak tartare, steamed halibut with Beluga caviar, Norwegian salmon, rack of lamb. Extensive wine list. A harpist entertains during Sunday brunch. This is the breakfast, lunch, and dinner restaurant of the hotel. Moderate prices.

Gumbo Shop, 630 St Peter St, French Quarter (tel. 525-1486). Good place to get acquainted with local dishes. There's a combination platter with ample portions of shrimp Creole, red beans and rice, and jambalaya.

Dining in a restored 1794 building and small patio. Open daily 11.00-23.00. Inexpensive.

Imperial Palace Regency, Poydras Plaza, CBD (tel. 522-8666). Stylish room with a seven-page menu of Hunan, Cantonese, and Szechuan dishes. The lemon chicken is divine. Exotic drinks include Fog Cutter and Missionary's Downfall. The only dress code is 'no shorts.' Inexpensive. Near the Superdome.

Isadora, 1100 Poydras St (suite 101 in the Energy Centre) (tel. 585-7787). A chic, 90-seat Art Deco restaurant with a popular cocktail lounge and nouvelle Continental/American cuisine. Two of the three chefs are Cajuns, so expect some robust touches to classic dishes. For starters you might try rabbit Wellington, then order a main dish of English mixed grill or tournedos with crawfish Sabayon and sauce Rouennaise. Jazz is on tap, too. Gentlemen are asked to wear jackets, and reservations are advised for dinner. Open for lunch and dinner; closed Sundays. Moderate. CBD.

Kabby's, Hilton Hotel (tel. 584-3880). A big, beautiful room with enormous windows that afford a smashing view of the Mississippi River. Seafood is the speciality, but there is a wide selection to choose from. For openers you might try catfish chips (thin slices of fried catfish); oysters Rockefeller; turtle soup or crawfish bisque. Entrées include whole broiled or steamed lobster; barbecued shrimp; steamed clams done

A Monday meal for Creoles: red beans and rice, with shrimp

up with white wine, butter, olive oil, basil, oregano, and thyme; roast duck with fruited wild rice and orange glaze; and *filet mignon*. Don't miss the peanut butter ice cream pie. Expensive. Reservations suggested. CBD.

K-Paul's Louisiana Kitchen, 416 Chartres St, French Quarter (tel. 942-7500). The best place for red-hot Cajun food. This is the kitchen of celebrity chef Paul Prudhomme, whose blackened redfish and other Cajun dishes have created a sensation around the world.

This is another place that takes no reservations, and there is usually a long queue waiting to get in. Once inside, the chances are that you will have to share a table. Décor is decidedly down-market; martinis are served in jelly glasses. Expensive. Lunch and dinner Monday to Friday; closed weekends.

Kolb's, 125 St Charles Ave, CBD (tel. 522-8278). Located in a historic landmark, this is a sprawling German-cum-Creole restaurant with lots of old-world charm. The antique ceiling fans are cranked by little mechanical men in lederhosen. Oktoberfest is celebrated with 'oom-pah-pah' bands and great gusto. The restaurant is on a prime corner for Mardi Gras parades, during which it has special prices for buffets and open bar. Open daily (dinner only on Sundays). Moderate prices.

La Madeleine, 547 St Ann St (tel. 568-9950). A fine people-watching spot on Jackson Square that serves breakfast, lunch and light dinners. Mouth-watering croissants are baked in a wood-burning oven, and they are the best in town. There is also a wide selection of pastries. Usually crowded. Open Monday to Thursday 07.00-20.00; Friday and Saturday till 21.00. Inexpensive. French Quarter.

La Marquise, 625 Chartres St (tel. 524-0420). A charming little French pastry shop with tables inside and in a small rear courtyard. A glass case is filled with delicious Napoleons, tarts, cream puffs, chocolate éclairs, and a wide assortment of diet-destroyers. There are also salads, but this is not really the place to pop in if you are on a serious diet. Very popular with locals. Open every day of the week from 07.30 till 17.30. Inexpensive. French Quarter.

Le Bistro, 733 Toulouse St (tel. 528-9206). The tiny but very elegant eatery of the Hotel Maison de Ville has the décor

Mr B's staff offer a friendly welcome to Mr B's Bistro, where prices are quite friendly, too

and ambience of a turn-of-the-century Parisian bistro. The menu is limited but imaginative, with offerings such as 'grilled practically boneless rabbit' in Dijon brandy cream, and grilled duck breast with pepper jelly glaze. The tables are a little too close together, and the noise level is high. Be sure to reserve a table for dinner; there are only 40 seats, and they are much in demand. Jackets are required at dinner. Open for lunch and dinner. Expensive. French Quarter

Mother's, 401 Poydras St, CBD (tel. 523-9656). Great breakfast place, crowded very early with CBD blue-collar workers,

chicken and andouille. Desserts are elaborate concoctions. Extensive wine list. Moderate prices. Lunch and dinner daily.

Palm Court Jazz Café, 1204 Decatur St (tel. 525-0200). This new and innovative addition to the restaurant scene is the creation of George H Buck, Jr and his Yorkshire-born wife, Nina. The charming café, with old-brick walls, tile floors, second-line parasols, and ceiling fans, is actually in the warehouse of the GHB Jazz Foundation Building. The Foundation operates eight record labels devoted to jazz, folk, blues, and other American sounds. Jazzology Records is the world's oldest independent jazz record label. You can request your favourite record and listen as you dine on shrimp Creole, steak and mushroom pie, jambalaya, chicken Provençal, and other offerings, including fine desserts. The café also acts as an information centre to visitors from around the world, offering suggestions about where to find the best live jazz in the city. Open Wednesdays, Thursdays and Sundays 11.00-22.00; Fridays and Saturdays noon till 23.00. Closed Mondays and Tuesdays. Very inexpensive. French Quarter.

Rib Room, Royal Orleans Hotel (tel. 529-7045). A cosy old brick room with big windows overlooking Royal Street, the Rib Room's special dish is prime rib of beef and Yorkshire pudding. However, there is a long *à la carte* menu,

but the speciality here is the po-boy. Hams and roasts are baked on the premises. Good red beans and rice, too. Mother's has been going strong more than 50 years. Open Tuesday to Saturday, 05.00-22.00 (closed Sundays and Mondays). Very inexpensive.

Mr B's Bistro, 201 Royal St, French Quarter (tel. 523-2078). Many of the seafood and steak dishes are cooked on a hickory grill, and an enticing aroma wafts out into the street. Classy rooms with etched glass, polished wood, and a grand piano for evening music and brunches (Saturday and Sunday). If you are not fond of seafood but want to try gumbo (which usually features sea creatures), try Gumbo Ya-Ya, which is made here with

FOOD AND DRINK

and if you have difficulty making up your mind opt for the assortment of roast beef, roast pork, and leg of lamb. Beef, game, and fowl sizzle on the slowly revolving rotisserie at one end of the room; desserts are rolled out on a silver cart. Things are less pricey at lunch, and you will need a reservation for dinner. Open daily for lunch and dinner. Expensive. French Quarter.

St Ann's Deli, 800 Dauphine St (tel. 529-4421). One of the busiest spots in town, and open 24 hours a day. Breakfast is served anytime except between 11.30 and 14.00. There is an extensive menu of sandwiches, muffulettas, omelettes, salads, and plate lunches such as barbecue spare ribs, fried chicken, lasagne, and so on. Their home-made desserts are wonderful, and the carrot cake is a French Quarter favourite. Free delivery anywhere in the Quarter.

Sazerac, Fairmont Hotel, CBD (tel. 529-4733). Until recently the Sazerac was a wonderfully schmaltzy and romantic ruby-red room with velvet walls and strolling accordionist. But the room has had a facelift, and everything has changed, including the chef. The cuisine is continental with nouvelle Creole touches, and while there are still *à la carte* listings, reasonably priced *table d'hôte* menus are offered for lunch and dinner. A classical harpist has replaced the strolling accordionist, and the old-world aura has gone

with the wind. Jackets required for dinner. Dramatic food presentations (caviar is rolled out in a magnificent ice-carving). Open daily. Very expensive for dinner; moderate for lunch.

SEB's, JAX Brewery, French Quarter (tel. 522-1696). An enormous, stylish room wrapped in windows that afford splendid views of the Mississippi River. Seafood is king here (13 varieties of fish are on the menu), prepared in lighter-than-usual Creole sauces. Open daily (closed Saturdays at lunch). Moderate.

Tujaques, 823 Decatur St, French Quarter (tel. 525-8676). Pronounced 'two jacks,' this atmospheric restaurant is evocative of old New Orleans. Hardly surprising, since it's the second oldest restaurant in town, having been established more than 150 years ago. Classic Creole dishes are served; six-course dinners are served nightly. Open for lunch daily. Moderate.

Winston's, Hilton Hotel (tel. 561-0500). This sophisticated restaurant is one of the best hotel dining rooms in town. Prime rib of roast beef, served with horseradish sauce, comes to you on a silver cart. Porterhouse and *filet mignon* are among the steaks listed, and other entrées include Veal Oscar; Long Island duckling topped with Grand Marnier sauce; and Lobster Savoy (whole live Maine lobster sautéed in a saffron cream sauce). Desserts are also divine. Dinner only, expensive. CBD.

SHOPPING

Shopping options here are almost endless. French Quarter shops range from little bazaars to glittering indoor malls such as the Jackson Brewery Corporation's **JAX Brewery**, the **Millhouse**, and the **Marketplace**. The **French Market**, on the site of a 17th-century trading post, runs along Decatur and North Peters Streets, filled with souvenir shops and open-air cafés with toe-tapping jazz. Sophisticated **Royal Street** is world-renowned for its antique stores.

Shopping can be relaxed and colourful in the Crescent City

SHOPPING

In the CBD, **Canal Place** is a smart mall with market stores such as Laura Ashley, Saks Fifth Avenue, Gucci, Brooks Brothers, and F A O Schwartz. **Riverwalk**, trailing upriver from Spanish Plaza, is a jazzy indoor festival marketplace with more than 200 shops and restaurants. Near the Superdome, the **New Orleans Center** houses a plethora of stores, including Lord & Taylor and Macy's.

Upriver, **Magazine Street** is a 6-mile (9½km) stretch of antique shops in tiny shotgun houses and once grand Victorian mansions. Wicker, bric-a-brac, ancient dishes and glassware, and second-hand clothes are featured in most of the shops. The New Orleans Welcome Center provides a free guide to Magazine Street's shops and restaurants, and the Magazine Street bus runs right up to them. If you want to make the most out of Magazine Street (and Royal Street), contact local antiques expert Macon Riddle (tel. 899-3027). She conducts personalised guided tours and may be able to put you in touch with your dream antique.

The Rink, with only a few shops, was built in 1884 as the Crescent City Roller Rink, one of the South's first roller-skating rinks. It is in the Garden District at 2727 Prytania Street, reached by taking the St Charles Streetcar, getting off at Washington Avenue, and walking one block towards the River. Further upriver, **Riverbend's** boutiques, toy shops, and

Once an Indian trading post, the renovated French Market is still a popular part of the city

eateries are in little Creole houses nestling by the bend in the Mississippi. Hampson, Maple, and Dante are the main shopping streets in this area, and the St Charles Streetcar runs right past it.

Uptown Square is a small shopping centre with medieval-style buildings surrounding a village square. Locally-owned shops purveying gifts and novelties are located here. You can

chicory coffee, beignet mix, and packaged local foods are popular 'take-home' items. Carnival masks, jazz records and tapes, nostalgia clothing, custom-blended perfumes, New Orleans cookery books and local lore, and exquisite 17th- and 18th-century antiques are also prominent.

Listed below are some souvenir ideas and the best places to seek them out.

European and American Antiques:

British Antiques, 5415 Magazine St.

French Antique Shop, 225 Royal St.

Leon Irwin Antiques, 1800 Magazine St.

Manheim Galleries, 403-409 Royal St.

Moss Antiques, 411 Royal St.

Rothschild's Antiques, 241 Royal St and 321 Royal St.

Waldhorn Company, 343 Royal St.

Carnival Masks:

Hidden Images, 523 Dumaine St.

Rumors, 513 Royal St.

Tim Steele Masks, 1023 N Peters St.

Cookery Books and Other New Orleans Books:

DeVille Books & Prints, Riverwalk and JAX Brewery.

Librarie, 823 Chartres St.

Maple Street Book Shop, 7523 and 7529 Maple St.

New Orleans School of Cooking, JAX Brewery.

Chicory Coffee and Beignet Mix:

Café du Monde, 1039 Decatur St.

Aunt Sally's, French Market.

Custom-Blended Perfumes:

reach it by taking the St Charles Streetcar to Broadway and transferring to the Broadway bus.

The city also has sprawling concrete malls with cinema, chain stores, hardware stores, and much more.

As in any major tourist attraction New Orleans has a bizarre assortment of useless trinkets. However, this unique city also offers a variety of unusual souvenirs, most of which are related, not surprisingly, to food, jazz, and Mardi Gras.

In the food category, pralines,

SHOPPING

Bourbon French Perfumes, 525
St Ann St.
Hové Parfumeur, 824 Royal St.
Food:
Gumbo Ya-Ya, 219 Bourbon St.
Louisiana Products, 507 St Ann
St.
Jazz Records and Tapes:
Canal Record Center, 1012
Canal St.
Record Ron's, 1129 Decatur St.
Werlein's, 605 Canal St.
Millinery:
Fleur de Paris, 712 Royal St.
Yvonne La Fleur, 8131

*Near the Riverwalk centre and its
200-plus shops and restaurants, a
fruit stall keeps to a simpler style*

Hampson St and Riverwalk.
Pralines:
Laura's, 115 Royal St.
Old Town Praline Shop, 627
Royal St.
In 1988, Louisiana became the
first state in the United States to
create a sales tax refund
system for foreign tourists. The
new law became effective 1
January, 1989, and provides for
state and local sales tax
exemptions on the purchase of
tangible personal property
bought by foreign travellers.
Cash refunds or cheques will
be given to tourists when they
leave the state for their home
countries.

The swimming pool of the Landmark French Quarter Hotel

ACCOMMODATION

New Orleans offers a wide variety of accommodation, ranging from small European-style guesthouses filled with antiques, to spartan chain motels, to high-tech convention hotels. Virtually all have courtyards awash with subtropical plants and flowers; many are balconied; and almost all have a swimming pool.

The greatest concentration of hotels is in the French Quarter and the CBD, but the Garden District has some fine properties, as well.

New Orleans Bed and Breakfast can put you in a private home, an apartment or a condominium. There are more than 300 properties to choose from, at prices ranging from $35-$150. Write to Sarah-Margaret Brown, PO Box 8163, New Orleans, LA 70182.

The following accommodations are grouped according to type. Hotels offer full services (restaurants, cocktail lounge, room service, etc). Guesthouses are often family operations offering fewer services, but a friendlier atmosphere. Motels are 'drive-in' hotels, usually with restaurant, bar, and so on. Price categories fall into the

ACCOMMODATION

following categories: over $150 – Expensive; $90 to $150 – Moderate; and below $90 – Inexpensive (prices may, of course, change). Hotel rates are doubled during Mardi Gras.

Hotels

Bourbon Orleans, 717 Orleans Street, New Orleans, LA 70116 (tel. 523-2222). Just a block from Jackson Square, this balconied hotel has 211 rooms, including several split-level suites, with Queen Anne furnishings and canopied beds. Massive white doors on Orleans Street open to a splendid white lobby with crystal chandeliers. Spiral stairs lead from the lobby to the Orleans Ballroom, which dates from 1815 and was the scene of elaborate *bals masques*. French Quarter. Expensive.

Chateau Motor Hotel, 1001 Chartres Street, New Orleans, LA 70116 (tel. 524-9636). Nothing fancy, but an excellent, inexpensive choice in the 'lower Quarter' (below Jackson Square). Well-maintained rooms, which vary in size, are furnished either with traditional décor or with antiques. The charming little outdoor café is just a few steps from the pool. French Quarter. Inexpensive.

Dauphine Orleans Hotel, 415 Dauphine St, New Orleans, LA 70112 (tel. 586-1800). A wide variety of rooms is available, including some luscious suites, and all are equipped with mini-bars and cable TV. Continental breakfast is taken in a bright,

cheerful breakfast room, and each guest receives a morning newspaper. There is a guest library; and an exercise room with a Jacuzzi. French Quarter. Moderate to expensive.

Fairmont Hotel, University Place, New Orleans, LA 70140 (tel. 529-7111). Luxurious hotel with lots of gilded pillars, crystal chandeliers and scarlet carpeting. There are more than 700 rooms, all of which are deluxe, with down pillows, electric shoe buffers, and a variety of frills. Several sizes of suites are available, including those with two bedrooms, living room, dining room, fully-equipped kitchen, and service area. Among the four restaurants are Bailey's, open 24 hours; the Blue Room, one of the South's most famous supper clubs; and the Sazerac, which is extremely up-market. There's a gym, a pool, tennis courts, gift shops, and a concierge to fetch whatever you are unable to find. CBD.

Landmark Bourbon Street, 541 Bourbon St, New Orleans, LA 70130. Right in the middle of 'The Street,' this large facility has identically decorated rooms, facilities for the handicapped, non-smokers' rooms, a very inexpensive cafeteria, and lounges. There are rooms with balconies on Bourbon, but there are also two floors with public balconies where you can watch the action below and then retire to a quiet back room to sleep. French Quarter. Moderate.

Landmark French Quarter Hotel, 920 N Rampart St, LA

*New Orleans' top class menus
deserve top class surroundings*

70116 (tel. 524-3333). An
intimate hotel with tropical
courtyard, pool, restaurant,
lounge. Three blocks from
Bourbon Street. Moderate.
Le Meridien, 614 Canal St,
New Orleans, LA 70130 (tel.
525-6500). Air France's glitzy
$65 million addition to the hotel
scene is a marvel of pink
marble and all manner of
luxurious touches. In addition
to the cushy rooms and suites,
the hotel has a fully-equipped
health club, French haute
cuisine in Henri, casual (though
not cheap) dining in La
Gauloise, and dixieland nightly
in the lobby. Expensive. CBD.
Le Richelieu, 1234 Chartres St,
New Orleans, LA 70116. (tel.
529-2492). One of the best buys
in town. Stylish, individually
decorated rooms and suites
with brass ceiling fans, ironing
boards, and walk-in closets.
Some rooms have refrigerators.
Lovely courtyard with poolside
café. Free parking, friendly
staff. Inexpensive.
**Maison DeVille Hotel &
Cottages,** 727 Toulouse St,
New Orleans, LA 70130 (tel.
561-5858). One of the most
charming hotels in the city.

ACCOMMODATION

Furnished with 18th-century antiques, four-poster and canopied beds, and lovely pastel prints. Breakfast brought to you on a silver tray, sherry and afternoon tea served in the parlour. Tennessee Williams lived for a time in Number 9, just off the splendid courtyard. Separate from the main hotel, the super-deluxe Audubon Cottages offer every imaginable amenity. French Quarter. Expensive.

Marriott Hotel, 555 Canal St, New Orleans, LA 70140 (tel.581-1000). This large link in the ever-lengthening chain of Marriott hotels has more than 1,300 modern rooms in two sections: the 21-storey Quarter Tower and the 41-storey River Tower (in which there are luxury suites). There are three lounges and three restaurants, including the top-floor Riverview Restaurant, which has a Sunday jazz brunch and a spectacular view of the river. There is also a swimming pool, health club, and sauna. Expensive. CBD.

Monteleone, 214 Royal St, New Orleans, LA 70140 (tel. 523-3341). The French Quarter's oldest (and tallest) hotel celebrated its 100th birthday in 1986. A fourth generation of Monteleones operates the favourite home-away-from-home for many celebrities (Paul Newman among them). Handsome rooms, elegant suites, rooftop pool, gift shops, several restaurants and cafés. Splendid lobby chandeliers. Moderate to expensive.

New Orleans Hilton Riverside & Towers, Poydras St at the Mississippi River, New Orleans 70140 (tel. 561-0500). A smart hotel with a soaring atrium lobby, about a dozen restaurants, bars, and lounges, and lots of activity. This is one of the city's major convention hotels, and the Convention Center is just down the street. It's also perched just above Riverwalk, and the Riverfront Streetcar runs right by it. Pete Fountain's Club is here; so is the Rivercenter Racquet and Health Club, which offers all manner of fitness business. CBD.

Pontchartrain Hotel, 2031 St Charles Ave, New Orleans, LA 70140 (tel. 524-0581). Sedate and gracious, this deluxe hotel in the Garden District is a member of Preferred Hotels Worldwide. Hallmarks of the hotel are impeccable taste and attentive service. Rooms and suites are individually decorated; suites are the size of small houses. Lots of marble, polished wood, fresh flowers, chandeliers. No pool, courtyard or gym; merely simple elegance. On the St Charles Streetcar line. Garden District. Expensive.

The Sheraton New Orleans boasts a large lobby and over 1,000 rooms

Royal Orleans (Omni), 621 St Louis St, New Orleans, LA 70140 (tel. 529-5333). White marble, oriental rugs, exquisite statuary and handsome wall hangings greet you in the lobby of the Royal O. Rooms are decked out in custom-made furnishings and marble baths with phones (some suites have Jacuzzis). Heated rooftop pool, well-equipped exercise room, gift shops, and several bars, restaurants (the estimable Rib Room among them) and lounges, including the sophisticated Esplanade Lounge. French Quarter. Expensive.

Royal Sonesta, 300 Bourbon St, New Orleans, LA 70140 (tel. 586-0300). It seems like stepping on to another planet when you pass from the babble of Bourbon into the serene marbled lobby of the Sonesta. Rooms with balconies are noisy (naturally), but there are quiet ones overlooking the lush courtyard. Rooms are decorated in country French style with antique reproductions. Ample entertainment and restaurant facilities. French Quarter. Moderate to expensive.

Sheraton New Orleans Hotel, 500 Canal St, New Orleans, LA 70130 (tel. 525-2500). Another up-scale chain hotel, the Sheraton has a spacious lobby with a tropical lounge, boutiques, and a spiral staircase winding up to the Café Promenade on the second level. The 1,200-room facility includes non-smokers'

ACCOMMODATION

rooms and Tower Suites with concierge services and extra pampering. A special $79 rate for the standard rooms is occasionally offered, and if it is available you should snap it up. Moderate to Expensive. CBD.

Windsor Court, 300 Gravier St, New Orleans, LA 70140 (tel. 523-6000). James Coleman, Honorary British Consul-General, is the man behind this sumptuous all-suites hotel. It is built around his $5 million art collection, much of which pertains to the British royal family. The enormous lobby is usually filled with well-dressed folk. High tea with scones, finger sandwiches and chocolate truffles is served each afternoon at 16.00. The suites, in luscious pinks and greens, have bars, phones in every room, and many amenities. Fully-equipped health club, heated pool with underwater sound system. Stunning property. CBD. Expensive.

Guesthouses

French Quarter Maisonettes, 1120 Chartres St, New Orleans, LA 70116 (tel. 524-9918). Only seven units, almost always booked long in advance, built around an enormous courtyard. Accommodations are spacious and modestly furnished. Mrs Junius Underwood, the chatelaine, distributes an informative brochure to her guests with helpful advice about sightseeing, etc. No pool, no restaurant, and no phones in the rooms. Closed in July. French Quarter. Inexpensive.

Josephine Guest House, 1450 Josephine St, New Orleans, LA 70130 (tel. 524-6361). Oriental rugs on polished hardwood floors and French antiques offer a glimpse of Creole life in 19th-century New Orleans. Only six rooms. The mansion was built in 1870 and has been lovingly restored. In the morning a Creole breakfast is served to guests. Charming and gracious. Garden District.

Lamothe House, 621 Esplanade Ave, New Orleans, LA 70116 (tel. 947-1161). On the fringe of the Quarter, this pretty pink double townhouse is filled with a stunning collection of Victorian antiques. A variety of accommodations is available (main house, carriage house, slave quarters), with each room having its distinctive personality. Complimentary continental breakfast is served in a formal dining room or in the courtyard. No other meals are served, but wine and port are taken in the afternoons in the elegant parlour. Adjacent to the Quarter. Moderate to expensive.

Olivier House, 828 Toulouse St, New Orleans, LA 70112 (tel. 525-8456). Built in 1836 as a townhouse for a Mme Olivier, this charmer is a special favourite with Europeans, touring companies playing the Saenger, and top-name opera stars. The guesthouse is built around three lush courtyards, in one of which there is a small pool. Owned and operated by the friendly Danner family, the guesthouse has 40 rooms, some of which are filled with

A 19th-century mansion turned guesthouse; Lamothe House

exquisite antiques. There are also modern rooms and lovely suites. Near Bourbon Street in the French Quarter. Inexpensive to expensive. **Park View Guest House**, 7004 St Charles Ave, New Orleans, LA 70118 (tel. 861-7564). A historic 1884 Victorian mansion, replete with verandah and leaded glass doors, overlooking Audubon Park. Handsome carved armoires and four-posters, brass beds, and lots of charm. Some rooms share a bath. Complimentary continental breakfast is served beneath the house's original Waterford

ACCOMMODATION

chandelier. Comfortable TV lounge where you can get to know the other guests. Uptown, on St Charles Streetcar route. Inexpensive.

St Charles Guest House, 1748 Prytania St, New Orleans, LA 70130 (tel. 523-6556). Just a block off St Charles Avenue, Dennis and Joanne Hilton's guesthouse is simple, comfortable and affordable. They offer special rates to students and backpackers (the small 'backpacker' rooms share a bath and are not air-conditioned; not a good place to be in the summer). Continental breakfast, included in the rate, is served daily. Pool and sundeck. A good buy for those on a tight budget. Lower Garden District. Inexpensive.

Soniat House, 1133 Chartres St, New Orleans, LA 70116 (tel. 522-0570). Mr and Mrs Rodney Smith have decorated their guesthouse with antiques they collected during more than a quarter of a century of world travel. Among the considerable amenities are bath salts from Provence, Roger & Gallet soaps and bathside phones (some suites have Jacuzzis). Breakfast is brought to you on a silver tray, and there is an honour bar in the courtyard. French Quarter. Moderate to expensive.

Villa Convento, 616 Ursulines St, New Orleans, LA 70116 (tel. 522-1793). The Campo family, who can tell you anything you want to know about New Orleans, operates this three-storey Spanish-style guesthouse. Each of the rooms

is different in size and style; many have antiques and balconies. Ideal for families are rooms 305-306, where there is a bedroom and stairs leading to a twin-bedded loft. Continental breakfast can be taken on the leafy patio or in the breakfast room. French Quarter. Inexpensive to moderate.

Motels

Chateau LeMoyne Holiday Inn, 301 Dauphine St, New Orleans, LA 70112 (tel. 581-1303). This chain motel adapts well to its French Quarter location, with wrought-iron balconies, a lavish courtyard, and other typically New Orleans features. Immaculate rooms. Caters for families and business people, and offers special rates for senior citizens. Restaurant, lounge, pool. French Quarter. Moderate.

Days Inn-Downtown, 1630 Canal St, New Orleans, LA 70112 (tel. 586-0110). On the CBD shuttle route, this is a clean, comfortable motel with modest rooms and few frills. There are 230 rooms, including executive suites. There is a pool, restaurant, free parking, and laundry facilities. CBD.

Holiday Inn-Airport Holidome, Interstate 10 at Williams Blvd, Kenner, LA 70062 (tel. 467-5611). A good choice if you need to be near the airport. The new Holiday Inn trend is to build rooms around a dome where there is a pool, sauna, Jacuzzi, etc. Free parking; restaurant; lounge; airport shuttle.

NIGHTLIFE AND ENTERTAINMENT

New Orleans Music

Jazz was born in New Orleans, and the beat goes on and on. Not at all confined to nighttime, the music can be heard on Bourbon Street almost any time of the day. Music is played all over town in sleek clubs, at jazz brunches, in Jackson Square, and on riverboats: almost anywhere, including street corners where anything from a lone trumpeter to a 10-piece band may blast off. New Orleans street musicians are some of the best

The Absinthe Bar comes to life late at night, along with many of the Bourbon Street haunts

in the world. So are the local high school bands that play in Mardi Gras parades.

But there is more to New Orleans music than jazz. Walking through the French Quarter you will hear rhythm and blues, rock and roll, Cajun music, zydeco (black Cajun music), ragtime piano, even traditional Irish music and the occasional bagpiper.

Here are some of the most popular bars and clubs to hear the music (and in some places dance to it).

NIGHTLIFE AND ENTERTAINMENT

Absinthe Bar, 400 Bourbon St (tel. 525-8108). Opens at noon and really gets revved up around midnight with R&B playing till dawn. French Quarter.

Blue Room, Fairmont Hotel (tel. 529-7111). Sophisticated supper club often featuring top-name entertainers. You can eschew supper and catch the show over a drink at the bar (cover charge $7 week nights, $9 weekends). CBD.

Benny's Bar, 738 Valence St (tel. 895-9405). Couldn't be more casual in this uptown spot for low-down blues. Uptown.

544 Club, 544 Bourbon St (523-8611). A mixed bag of music, including traditional jazz. French Quarter.

Forty-One Forty-One, 4141 St Charles (tel. 891-9873). A classy split-level nightclub with a disco, occasional live music, and a clientele of mostly under-30's singles. St Charles

Streetcar.

Jimmy's, 8200 Willow St (tel. 861-8200). One of the hottest spots in town for hard rock. Mostly young college crowd. Uptown.

Mahogany Hall, 309 Bourbon St (tel. 525-5595). Stomping grounds of the famed Dukes of Dixieland, who are on the bandstand nightly except Sunday. French Quarter.

Sweet sounds in Preservation Hall

Maple Leaf, 8316 Oak St (tel. 866-5323). This is the place to dance to live Cajun music. Enormously popular with all ages. Uptown.

Pete Fountain's, Hilton Hotel, Poydras St (tel. 523-4374). One of the world's most famous clarinettists, New Orleans' own Pete Fountain performs in a plush red velvet room whenever he's at home. He tours a lot, so make sure you check before you book a table. CBD.

Preservation Hall, 726 St Peter St (tel. 522-2238 (day); 523-8939 (night). In a class of its own, the Hall is neither nightclub nor bar but merely the best place in the world to hear traditional jazz. Little in the way of creature comforts, but jazz legends play nightly from 20.30. French Quarter.

Storyville Jazz Hall, 1104 Decatur St (tel. 525-8199). A spacious place featuring local groups and occasional big names (in the latter case there is a $10-$15 cover charge). French Quarter.

Snug Harbor, 626 Frenchmen St (tel. 949-0696). One of the liveliest, most popular places in town. Café serves good burgers and steaks; bar upstairs. Cover charge of $3-$5 for the music. Fringe of the Quarter.

Tipitina's, 500 Napoleon Ave (tel. 897-3943). A New Orleans institution, Tip's attracts legions of locals as well as visiting celebrities. R&B, rock and roll, blues and occasional Cajun. This is where the estimable Neville Brothers perform when they're in town. Uptown.

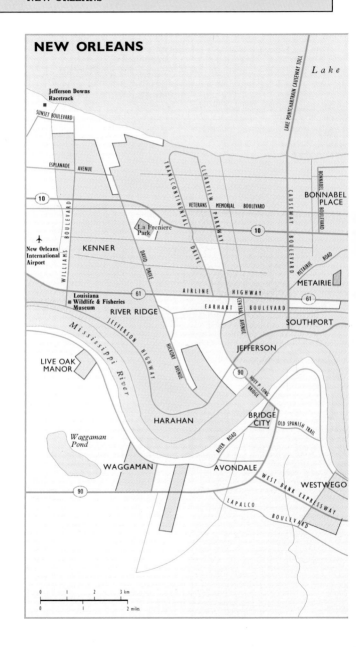

NEW ORLEANS

Lake Pontchartrain Causeway Toll

Lake

Jefferson Downs
Racetrack

SUNSET BOULEVARD

ESPLANADE AVENUE

BONNABEL
PLACE

BONNABEL BOULEVARD

10

WILLIAMS BOULEVARD

TRANSCONTINENTAL DRIVE

CLEARVIEW PARKWAY

VETERANS MEMORIAL BOULEVARD

CAUSEWAY BOULEVARD

10

La Freniere
Park

New Orleans
International
Airport

KENNER

DAVID DRIVE

METAIRIE ROAD

METAIRIE

61

AIRLINE HIGHWAY

61

Louisiana
Wildlife & Fisheries
Museum

RIVER RIDGE

EARHART BOULEVARD

CENTRAL AVENUE

SOUTHPORT

Mississippi River

JEFFERSON HIGHWAY

HICKORY AVENUE

JEFFERSON

LIVE OAK
MANOR

90

HUEY P. LONG BRIDGE

HARAHAN

BRIDGE
CITY

OLD SPANISH TRAIL

Waggaman
Pond

RIVER ROAD

WAGGAMAN

AVONDALE

WESTWEGO

90

WEST BANK EXPRESSWAY

LAPALCO BOULEVARD

0   1   2   3 km

0   1   2 miles

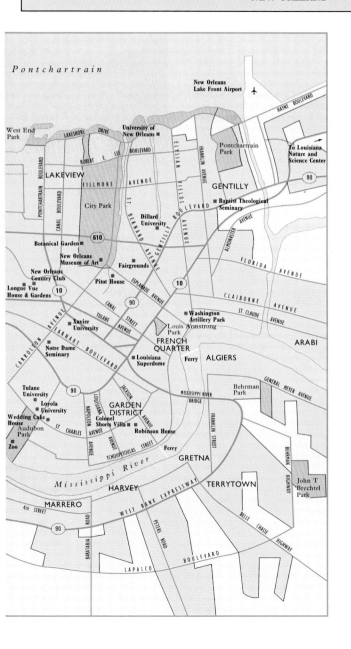

NIGHTLIFE AND ENTERTAINMENT

Jazz Brunches
Jazz brunches, a mix of New Orleans jazz and New Orleans food, are featured all over town. **Arnaud's**, 813 Bienville St and **Commander's Palace**, 1403 Washington Ave have the best jazz brunches, and are described more fully in the **Food and Drink** section.

Art Galleries
Bergen Galleries, 730 Royal St. The motto here is 'We have everything' and it seems to be true. There is a great selection of Mardi Gras and Jazz Fest posters.
Bryant Galleries, 524 Royal St. Established more than 25 years ago, Bryant has a collection of Haitian, European, and American fine arts, graphics, sculptures, glass, and primitives.
Dyansen Gallery, 433 Royal St. A stunning collection of Erté's sculpture, lithographs, seriographs, and gouaches is featured.
Gasperi Folk Art Gallery, 831 St Peter St. A collection of Southern regional folk art, including works by primitive artist Clementine Hunter.
Hanson Gallery, 229 Royal St. Contemporary master graphic and originals by Miro, Calder, Tamayo, Neiman and others.
Nahan Galleries, 540 Royal St. Master prints by internationally known artists. Publishers and agents for Toblasse, Papart, Bonti, and Agam.
Street Scene, 120 Riverwalk. Master carver Kay Glenn's creations depicting the plantations, peddlers, jazz

Two New Orleans specialities come together in several of the city's eating houses – jazz and brunch, a cross between breakfast and lunch

artists, and nuns of New Orleans.

Ballet
The **New Orleans City Ballet** (tel. 522-0996) is a company performing contemporary and classical ballets. Performances at the Theatre of the Performing Arts, Louis Armstrong Park, in September, December, March and May.

Bars

New Orleans has every kind of bar imaginable – be it topless, bottomless, jazz, historic, gay, piano, or oyster. The minimum legal drinking age is 21. You can buy packaged hard liquor, beer and wine in grocery stores and drugstores. There is no legal closing time, so bars can stay open until dawn. One bar doesn't even open till midnight, but many of them close at 01.00, and it is best to check before you begin any late bar-hopping.

The following is only a tiny selection:

Bayou Bar, Pontchartrain Hotel (tel. 524-0581). A casually chic piano bar. Long-time favourite of Uptowners and the celebrities who sometimes stay in the hotel. Uptown, on the St Charles Streetcar line.

Columns, Columns Hotel, St Charles Ave (tel. 899-9308). The verandah and cosy Victorian Bar are always crowded after 17.00 with business people who are accustomed to stopping off here on the way home.

Esplanade Lounge, Royal Orleans Hotel (tel. 529-5333). Sedate spot in the marbled halls of the Royal O. Soothing piano music, liqueurs, cocktails. French Quarter.

Jean Lafitte's Blacksmith Shop, 941 Bourbon St (523-0066). Dim and dark even during the day, this ancient bar, said to have been a front for Lafitte's illegal activities, is enormously popular with writers ranging from the unpublished to Pulitzer winners. At night, fans of Miss Lily Hood flock in to hear her sing at the piano bar. French Quarter.

Napoleon House, 500 Chartres St (524-9752). Peeling sepia walls, Napoleonic memorabilia, taped classical music, and muffulettas. This is arguably the most popular bar in town, especially with artists and writers. French Quarter.

Old Absinthe House, 240 Bourbon St (tel. 523-3181). A historic house with loyal clientele. French Quarter.

Pat O'Brien's, 718 St Peter St (tel. 525-4823). Birthplace of the Hurricane (you can buy a souvenir hurricane glass). There are three bars in this huge place, including a loud and lively piano bar and one of

the city's loveliest courtyards. Popular with college kids. French Quarter.

Que Sera, 3636 St Charles (tel. 897-2598). A pavement café whose Wednesday three-for-one (three drinks for the price of one) specials lure a huge crowd. St Charles Streetcar.

Sazerac Bar, Fairmont Hotel (tel. 529-7111). Elegant watering hole in the deluxe hotel, next to the restaurant of the same name. CBD.

Cruising along the Mississippi in an old-time riverboat, with its railed decks and great paddlewheel, is a unique Louisiana treat

Top of the Mart, World Trade Center (tel. 522-9795). A slowly revolving lounge on the 33rd floor of the WTC. A magnificent view (don't put your purse on the windowsill; it doesn't revolve!). CBD.

Concerts

The New Orleans Symphony Orchestra (tel. 525-0500), conducted by Maxim Shostakovich, presents a variety of programmes. In addition to its schedule of classical music concerts, there are family-orientated Discovery Concerts, open rehearsals, and kinder-konzerts for youngsters. Performances are at the Orpheum Theatre, University Place, CBD.

Dutch Alley in the French Market is the site of frequent free dixieland and jazz concerts. You can pick up a programme at the kiosk in Dutch Alley.

Opera

New Orleans was the first city in America in which opera was performed. Nationally acclaimed artists appear in productions mounted by the **New Orleans Opera Association** at the Theatre of the Performing Arts. For information about performances, call 529-2278.

Riverboats

Among the most popular attractions in New Orleans are the great white riverboats whose paddlewheels kick up froth on the Mississippi River. A variety of excursions are offered. The **Steamboat**

Natchez (tel. 586-8777), looking like a big floating wedding cake, beckons with her off-key steam whistles for two-hour harbour cruises and dinner-plus-jazz cruises. She docks at the Toulouse Street Wharf behind the Jax Brewery. The **Creole Queen** (tel. 524-0814) has daily cruises, as well as weekend dinner-plus-jazz outings with a sumptuous Cajun/Creole buffet and toe-tapping music. Departures are from the Riverwalk Poydras Street Wharf. The little **Cotton Blossom** (tel. 586-8777), also departing from Riverwalk, offers cruises to and from Audubon Zoo. The **Bayou Jean Lafitte** (tel. 586-8777) leaves from the Toulouse Street Wharf for 5-hour bayou cruises.

Sports

Bicycling You can rent bicycles at Bicycle Michaels (tel. 945-9505) for pedalling around the French Quarter and the CBD. You can also cycle around the tree-shaded City Park by renting bikes at the Park's Casino (tel. 483-9371).

Boating The Mississippi River Challenge Cup Race pits powerboats against each other for a race from New Orleans to St Louis. Don Johnson of TV's *Miami Vice* participates each year in the event, which takes place in September (tel. 314/367-3062). On the mossy lagoons in City Park you can rent canoes and paddleboats and drift out among the swans (tel. 483-9371).

Catamarans, sailboards, and powerboats can be rented for Lake Pontchartrain at Sailboats South (tel. 288-7245).

Canoeing and Tubing North of Lake Pontchartrain, the Bogue Chitto and Tangipahoa Rivers are wonderful waterways for canoeing and tubing. In New Orleans, outings and rentals are available at Canoe and Trail Adventures (tel. 833-9541).

Football If you are curious about American football, you can see good examples of

both professional and collegiate games at the colossal Superdome. Home games of the New Orleans Saints, a professional team in the National Football League, are played in the Dome (for ticket information tel. 522-2600). The season begins in early September and culminates in January with the Superbowl, the championship contest between the winners of the two NFL conferences. The Superbowl, always accompanied by plenty of publicity, is sometimes played in the Dome. Carnival season is going strong by Superbowl time, which means that the city is full of football fans, international media, carnival revellers and parties.

The Superdome is also the venue for the annual 1 January Sugar Bowl Classic, one of

The vast Louisiana Superdome

NIGHTLIFE AND ENTERTAINMENT

several hotly-contested college bowl games played on or around New Year's Day. A variety of events takes place in the city at Sugar Bowl time, including a basketball tournament and a marathon.

Golf In April professional golfers turn up for the USF&G Golf Classic, held at the Jack

City Park is one of the biggest parks in the country; its 1,500 acres include ample sporting facilities

Nicklaus English Turn on the West Bank (tel. 394-5294). Visitors can play at the 18-hole course in Audubon Park (tel. 861-9511), and on one of the four courses at City Park (tel. 283-3458).

Hiking You can rent backpacking equipment and sign up for trips that last from an overnight stay to a week at Canoe & Trail Adventures (tel. 833-9541). Backpacking hikes are also offered by the Louisiana Nature and Science Center (tel. 246-9381).

Horse Riding In New Orleans you cannot hire a horse and ride off alone. However, organised trail rides are offered in Audubon Park at Cascade Stables (tel. 891-2246) and in City Park at Equestrian Stable (tel. 282-6200).

Horse Racing Thoroughbreds race all year round in the city. From Thanksgiving to the end of April the action is at the Fairgrounds, the country's third-oldest track (tel. 943-2200). From April to November the scene shifts to Jefferson Downs (tel. 466-8521).

Running In April, the Crescent City Classic is a major event with thousands of participants running from Jackson Square headed to Audubon Park (tel. 861-8686). A unique event is the Witches Moonlight Run the night before Hallowe'en. There are several popular jogging sites in the city. The best is Audubon Park, where there is a 2-mile (3km) jogging track along Oak Alley, shaded by a canopy of oak trees. There are 18 exercise stations along the track. City Park is

also a good place for jogging.

Tennis In September or October, the Virginia Slims Tennis Tournament brings professional players to the UNO Lakefront Arena (tel. 286-7222).

There are plenty of places to play tennis. In City Park there are 39 courts at the Wisner Tennis Center (tel. 483-9383); and 10 courts in Audubon Park (tel. 865-8638).

Theatre

There are a number of amateur theatres, including local dinner theatres, and one house where touring professional companies appear. Some of the well-established theatres are:

Contemporary Arts Center (tel. 523-1216). Produces plays by new playwrights and experimental works. The CAC's Krewe of Clones give highly satirical, sometimes controversial, parades and performances during Mardi Gras.

Le Petit Theatre Du Vieux Carré (tel. 522-2081). Located in a historic French Quarter building, this is the country's oldest continuously operating community theatre. Quality plays are produced here, including those in the Children's Corner, and Le Petit is also the venue for several of the festivals. It is worth the price of admission to see this charming old place.

Saenger Performing Arts Center (tel. 524-0876). Presents top-name entertainers, road companies of Broadway shows, and, occasionally, a classic film.

NIGHTLIFE AND ENTERTAINMENT

Walking tours

Friends of the Cabildo (tel. 523-3939). Guided tours of the French Quarter. Meet at the Presbytere in Jackson Square; tours are conducted Tuesday to Saturday at 09.30 and 13.30, Sunday at 13.30. Price of the tour includes admission into at least two Louisiana State Museum buildings. The tour is half-price for senior citizens and students.

Jean Lafitte National Historical Park (tel. 589-2636). A variety of tours is offered, including a French Quarter Tour. Of special note is the Cemetery Tour, which is a 1½ hour's walk through St Louis Cemetery No 1, the oldest cemetery and the nearest one to the Quarter. The tour leaves every morning at 09.30 from the Park's Folk Life Center, 916-18 N Peters St, French

Jackson Square, where soldiers once drilled and executions took place

Market, French Quarter. The Park Rangers also offer tours of the Garden District. All the tours are free and take place daily except Christmas, New Year's Day and Mardi Gras. You must have a reservation for the Cemetery and Garden District tours, and for the latter you must pay your own Streetcar fare.

Heritage Tours (tel. 949-9805). New Orleans' famous sons and daughters include Lillian Hellman, Truman Capote, and John Kennedy Toole, whose *A Confederacy of Dunces* won a Pulitzer Prize. Many famous writers have lived and worked in the French Quarter, among them William Faulkner, John Dos Passos, Sherwood Anderson, and Tennessee Williams. Heritage Tours takes you for a stroll through the Quarter, pointing out the houses and haunts of artists and writers, with anecdotes into the bargain.

WEATHER AND WHEN TO GO

Without doubt, it is hot here in the summer. Temperatures often edge above the 32 degrees C (90 degrees F) mark and stay there for weeks. Humidity also is high. During

Natural habitats are recreated so that Audubon Zoo's 1,000 or so animals feel at home

the summer months (the hottest are June, July, and August), very few visitors come to town. In the summer, fluffy white clouds can suddenly darken and bring an unexpected downpour, but for the most part the summer showers are brief. Hurricane season is from June until the end of November, and the city is

sometimes buffeted by high winds and pelted with heavy rain. New Orleans is 110 miles (177km) inland from the coast, and since hurricanes lose force as they travel across land, the city is saved from the major brunt of the storms. There is occasional Uptown flooding, but never in the French Quarter, which is on the high ground.

Winters are impossible to predict. Local TV meteorologists are renowned for their mis-forecasting. In December, it can be 30 degrees C (85 degrees F) or 2

WEATHER AND WHEN TO GO

New Orleans street entertainment is in a class of its own; the city is full of jazz, from the clubs and cafés to the pavements

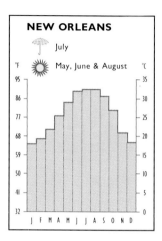

NEW ORLEANS

July

May, June & August

the two coldest months, are 7 degrees C (45 degrees F) to 10 degrees C (50 degrees F). In the winter it is always easy to distinguish between a local and a northern visitor. The visitor is running around in jogging shorts and tank top, while the local is shivering in boots, mittens, and ski-mask. Five degrees C (40 degrees F) can feel sharply cold here, because of the high humidity and the wind whipping off the Mississippi. However, it can also be 27 degrees C (80 degrees F), so you may need a T-shirt or a heavy coat; it is impossible to predict.

Spring is a glorious time of the year. By mid-March, azaleas are in full, beautiful bloom and the city is full of all manner of subtropical plants and flowers. April is a splendid time to visit New Orleans. May sizzles with the Jazz Fest, and temperatures and humidity are also often on the steamy side.

degrees C (35 degrees F) with a wind-chill factor 10 degrees lower. The average highs for January and February, usually

WEATHER AND WHEN TO GO

What to Wear

The Quarter has a colourful, costumed cast of characters, including Merlin the Magician and Ruthie the Duck Lady, which means you can wear almost anything and get away with it. There are, of course, sophisticated restaurants here that require proper attire (usually meaning no shorts or jeans). But in the summer (winter, too, depending upon the temperature), streetwear, especially in the Quarter, is of the sandals, halter-top and shorts variety. And, of course, the occasional pirate outfit and Indian head-dress. Local hoteliers and restaurateurs, being veterans of Mardi Gras, have seen many things and are virtually unshockable.

If you come in the summer (when many hotels slash their prices in order to attract visitors), bring lightweight clothing. Cotton may not travel as well as crushable synthetics, but it is considerably cooler. Women should bring a couple of cotton dresses for dining in up-market restaurants, and men need lightweight slacks and jacket. Some restaurants require a tie. Apart from that, bring the most comfortable, casual clothes you own. Shoes, especially, should be comfortable for walking. Some French Quarter pavements are cracked and play havoc with high heels. Riverboat decks are also unfriendly to heels. Unpredictable winters, of course, present a wardrobe problem. Women might bring a wool suit, which can be worn with either a heavy sweater or a cool blouse. For men, a lightweight wool suit should do. An ideal solution for men and women is an all-weather coat with a zip-out wool lining. Whatever time of year you come, bring sunglasses, a camera, a bag for maps and brochures, and an umbrella.

Mardi Gras – when even the most sober citizens let themselves go

HOW TO BE A LOCAL

There are several New Orleans shibboleths and any number of linguistic idiosyncracies.

It is entirely appropriate for songwriters to use 'New Orleens' in order to fit rhythm and rhyme. However, you almost have to have been born here to say the name of the city properly, and the pronunciation is virtually unprintable. You barely touch on the 'New,' stress the 'Or' (but pronounce it 'awe') and let the rest trail off: 'N'Awlins'. But locals do say 'Orleens' when referring to the street and the parish of that name.

Names of streets also have their own peculiar pronunciations. Chartres is 'charters'; Conti is 'con-tie';

In the 1900s the streetcar was just transport. Now it is a Historic Landmark, a commuter convenience, and an ideal way to sightsee

Burgundy is 'bur-*gun*-dy'; Clio is 'ca-*lie*-oh' (or the letters C L and the number 10: CL-10); and Tchoupitoulas is 'Chop-a-*too*-lus.'

Oysters are 'ersters', and the Central Business District is always referred to as the CBD. Never say 'Mardi Gras Day,' which would be like saying Fat Tuesday Day. The words 'carnival' and 'Mardi Gras' are not interchangeable; Carnival season begins in January and culminates in Mardi Gras, the last two weeks of the season. You will also be committing a *faux pas* if you refer to 'King Rex,' instead of Rex, King of Carnival.

HOW TO BE A LOCAL/SPECIAL EVENTS

When doubloons come showering through the air from the Mardi Gras floats and land on the pavement, step on one first before reaching a bare hand down to pick it up. This has little to do with protocol; it avoids broken hands.

The Jazz and Heritage Festival is always called the 'Jazz Fest'. Going to the market to buy food is known as 'making groceries.'

Refer to the strip of land running down the centre of a boulevard as the neutral ground, and call the trolley that runs down the neutral ground a streetcar. When you board the St Charles Streetcar, stand at the rear window – the only place which gives a good view of the street signs, which are planted in the neutral ground. There is also a better general view from the back, which is the front of the car when it travels back downtown.

SPECIAL EVENTS

January

New Orleans Classical Music Festival. Festivals focus not only on European composers, but put the spotlight on American musical comedy composers, such as Rodgers and Hammerstein; George Gershwin; and Cole Porter.

February/March
Mardi Gras

Taking nothing away from the spectacular festivities elsewhere, Mardi Gras in New Orleans, held in February or March, is the biggest festival in all of North America. Not for nothing is it called 'the greatest free show on earth.'

Carnival season begins each year on 6 January, Twelfth Night, and ends at midnight on Mardi Gras (Fat Tuesday). The final two weeks of the season are also referred to as Mardi Gras, and the last four days can only be called sheer madness.

There are about 60 Carnival organisations, called krewes, that stage elaborate public parades and private balls. Lundi Gras, or Fat Monday, is a free, public masked ball which takes place in Spanish Plaza the night before Fat Tuesday. Extravagant floats, animated, illuminated, and loaded with masquers roll throughout the city, accompanied by dixieland bands, high-stepping marching bands, horsemen in plumed helmets and flowing robes of satin and velvet, clowns and flambeau-carriers (torch-bearers).

In New Orleans, there is no such thing as a parade spectator. The float-riders toss souvenirs, called 'throws,' into the crowds lining the parade routes. The throws include cups, bikinis and doubloons (aluminium 'coins'), but by far the most popular are the beads. Cheap plastic beads, which cause otherwise sane people to shriek, jostle and scramble. All during Mardi Gras beads are worn like badges of courage, which in a way they are.

The only souvenir more coveted than the beads are the gilded coconuts handed out by the exotic Zulu Social Aid & Pleasure Club, which is the first parade on the last day. Rex, King of Carnival, parades with his krewe after Zulu, followed by a couple of hundred decorated trucks. By mid-morning crowds throng Canal Street and Bourbon Street, many wearing gorgeous, sometimes totally outrageous, costumes. Bourbon Street balconies are jammed with people who booked far enough in advance to get a room overlooking the action.

Mardi Gras fever grips the crowds

SPECIAL EVENTS

The last parade of the day is Comus, the first Mardi Gras krewe, organized in 1857. At precisely midnight, mounted police with megaphones begin easing through the mass of humanity on Bourbon Street, proclaiming that 'Mardi Gras is over.' At the stroke of midnight Ash Wednesday ushers in the Lenten season. To calculate the date of Mardi Gras, count back 46 days from Easter.

March
Tennessee Williams New Orleans Literary Festival.

Takes place in mid-March and salutes the Pulitzer Prize-winning playwright, who wrote *A Streetcar Named Desire* in an apartment on St Peter Street. Events include a writers' conference, theatrical performances and parties.

April
French Quarter Festival, on the second weekend in April, is an all-out celebration with food and jazz. Spring Fiesta begins the first Friday after Easter with a 'Night in Old New Orleans' parade. A lovely time to visit New Orleans.

jambalaya, red beans and rice, and other New Orleans specialities while listening to the music. Second only to Mardi Gras in popularity.

July
New Orleans Food Festival, in early July, takes place in the Rivergate Exhibition Center, where chefs from all over the city provide 'tasters' of their specialities. La Fete (The National Festival of Food and Cookery) has food-related events taking place all over the city.

October
Festa D'Italia is the big Italian festival, with parades and parties. The Louis Armstrong Festival is a tribute to native son 'Satchmo.' Plenty of jazz. Hallowe'en, 31 October, is a major event here, with elaborate costumes, masked balls, and events such as the Witches Moonlight Run.

December
A Creole Christmas, during the entire month. Papa Noel (the Creole Santa Claus) arrives on a riverboat; parades; special children's events; house museums dressed in 19th-century Christmas finery; candlelight and Christmas carols in Jackson Square. Hotels offer special Papa Noel rates during the month, and restaurants prepare special Reveillon menus. Bonfires on the Levee is a Christmas Eve tradition in nearby St James Parish. Residents on both sides of the river build giant bonfires which light the way for Papa Noel.

Festivals are a way of life in New Orleans, where every opportunity is taken to dress up, play jazz and, as the Cajun saying goes, let the good times roll!

Everything is in blossom, and Fiesta tours take you into private homes and courtyards. New Orleans Jazz & Heritage Festival, during the last weekend in April and first weekend in May, draws musicians from all over the world for round-the-clock celebrations. On weekends the in-field of the Fairgrounds is filled with music and food tents, where you can feast on

CHILDREN

Audubon Zoo (see **What to See**) and the City Park's Storyland and amusement park are good places for children, and clowns are almost always up to their antics in Jackson Square and around the French Market. Kinderkonzerts are performed by the New Orleans Symphony Orchestra, and Le Petit Theatre's Children's Corner has several productions during the year. The **Louisiana Children's Museum** has hands-on exhibits, including a mini-market (for 'making groceries,') a make-believe clinic; and a variety of other exhibits.

The **Louisiana Nature and Science Center** offers swamp exhibits, nature walks, and canoe excursions; and **Musée Conti Wax Museum**, New Orleans' answer to Madame Tussaud's, has exhibits and life-like figures in scenes depicting the city's history and legends. **Ripley's Believe It Or Not Museum** is a collection of oddities from Robert Ripley's aptly-named Odditorium.

New Orleans for Kids is a colouring book put out by the Tourist Commission to educate and entertain children; available at the New Orleans Welcome Center.

Other venues ideal for children are:
Blaine Kern's Mardi Gras World, 233 Newton St, Algiers (tel. 362-8211). For a treat only available in New Orleans, take the free ferry at the foot of Canal Street, turn right as you exit the landing, and stroll along the levee till you come to the huge warehouses (called 'dens') in which fantastic floats are created for 40 of the Carnival krewes. Blaine Kern operates the world's largest float-building outfit, and it is a veritable Santa's workshop where you can watch the artists and craftsmen at work. Children (and adults) love having their pictures taken with some of the fabulous

Children are well catered for in New Orleans' parks and playgrounds

figures mounted on the floats.
Open Monday to Friday
09.30-16.00; admission is $3.50
for adults, $2.50 for children.
**Louisiana State Railroad
Museum,** 519 Williams Blvd,
Kenner (tel. 468-7223). 'See and
Feel' displays give children a
glimpse of old-time steam
locomotives. There are model
trains, cut-outs of train routes,
films, photographs, and slide
shows. The museum is open
Tuesday to Saturday
09.00-17.00 and Sunday
13.00-17.00. Admission is $1 for
adults, 50 cents for children
under 12.

TIGHT BUDGET

The most economic way to
travel is with an organised tour
group. Some people would
rather not give up certain
freedoms (where and when to
eat, for example), while others
are delighted to have
everything, including tips,
taken care of. The following
tips are for those travelling
independently:
Instead of a taxi or limousine,
take the bus that runs between
the airport and the CBD. The
fare is $1.10, and the trip takes
about an hour.

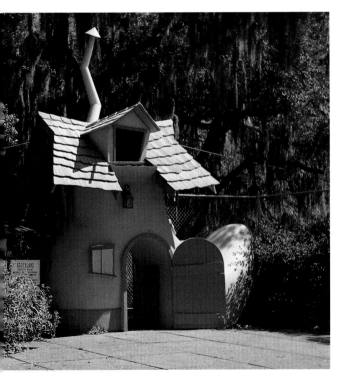

TIGHT BUDGET

If you are operating on a shoestring, ask if accommodation is available at the **Marquette House** (a youth hostel with rock-bottom rates). The **YMCA** at Lee Circle has accommodation for both men and women, and while the rooms are spartan you do have the advantage of the pool and the well-equipped gym.

Do your sightseeing by bus and streetcar (on foot in the French Quarter). The fare is 30 cents for the CBD shuttle; 60 cents for all other buses and streetcars. A 5-cent transfer coupon allows you to make four changes, so if you plan wisely you can cover a lot of territory for 65 cents.

The New Orleans Museum of Art is free all day Thursday, and can be reached by bus. The city is full of inexpensive eating places. A full breakfast at Esmeralda's in the French Quarter costs about $2. At Café du Monde, open 24 hours a day, there are three beignets to an order, and that with coffee will cost $1.85 (including tax). For lunch, do as many locals do: stop by the Central Grocery Store on Decatur Street, pick up a muffuletta and a beer, and eat them on Moon Walk down by the Mississippi (cost around $7). Or take the streetcar to the Camellia Grill, a favourite counter coffee shop, where you can get hot lunches for about $5. Ask at your hotel or at the New Orleans Welcome Center about other inexpensive eateries.

On Bourbon Street, the doors of jazz joints are flung open and music pours out, while children tapdance in the middle of the street. For only $2 you can listen to four hours of the best traditional jazz at Preservation Hall.

It is possible to eat well and cheaply in the Café du Monde

DIRECTORY
Arriving

Visitors will require a valid passport and visa, except in the case of British or Canadian citizens visiting for up to 90 days and holding a return ticket. In these instances a passport only is required. However, rules at city gateways vary about transit stops and visitors may not be able to re-enter the US after a visit outside the US without a visa.

If you are travelling independently, look into the low-cost APEX fares. Major airlines with scheduled flights to New Orleans include American Airlines, Continental Airlines and Delta Airlines. Remember that flights and fares can change rapidly.

You will arrive at New Orleans International Airport, also

International business and consulates are housed in the 33-floor World Trade Center

called Moisant Field. The sprawling airport is located 12 miles (20km) west of New Orleans in the town of Kenner, 20 to 30 minutes from downtown and the French Quarter, depending upon traffic. There are bars and lounges for travellers.

The journey into town can be made by taxi or Airport Rhodes Limousine. The taxi and limousine stands are just outside the baggage claim area. If you opt for a cab, be prepared to pay $18 for up to three passengers, and $6 for each additional person in your party. The Rhodes limousines are actually minivans (cost from $7 per person) that drop passengers off at all the hotels,

which means that it may take a while for you to reach your destination (if you share a taxi with three people in the taxi line, the driver will probably charge each of you the $7 airport limo rate). Airport Rhodes has a 24-hour reservation service (tel. 469-4555). An express bus service also operates from the airport to the Louisiana Transit Company terminal near the Civic Center. Major car rental agencies also have desks at the airport (see **Car Hire**).

Camping
In a wooded area off the Westbank Expressway, near

Bourbon Street, in the French Quarter – the heart of New Orleans

the Huey P Long Bridge (about a half hour from downtown), **Bayou Segnette State Park** has 100 sites with full hook-ups, tent pads, picnic tables and barbecue grills, comfort stations, laundromats, dump stations, pay telephones, and boat launch. Cost is $9 per night, and reservations are not necessary. The park also has furnished cabins with cooking utensils and bed linens (you have to bring your own towels and tin openers). The cabins, which sleep six to eight people, cost $50 per night, and you must reserve in advance: 1201 Bayou Segnette Ave, Westwego, LA 70094 (tel. 436-1107).

KOA West is a well-maintained campsite with 103 big back-in sites and full hook-ups ($24 per night), 15 tent sites ($20 per night), a pool, convenience store, laundry, playground and games room. It is located about 20 minutes west of downtown, and you need a reservation: 219 Starrett Rd, River Ridge, LA 70123 (tel. 467-1792). More information about camping can be obtained by writing to the Louisiana Office of State Parks, PO Drawer 1111, Baton Rouge, LA 70821 (tel. 925-3930) and Kampgrounds of America, Inc (KOA), PO Box 30558, Billings, Montana 59114.

Car Breakdown

If your car breaks down, lift the bonnet, tie a white handkerchief, or something white, to the door handle on the driver's side, get into the car, lock the doors, and wait for help. Major highways are well-patrolled, and a highway patrol car may appear. Drivers of 18-wheeler trucks will sometimes stop for distressed motorists, and they can summon help via CB radio. The American Automobile Association has a reciprocal agreement with all AIT clubs. You may want to call AAA Louisiana before taking to the road: 3445 N Causeway, Metairie (tel. 838-7500). A towing service is provided by **Jay Paul Roussell Gulf Service** (tel. 568-1177) and **Star/Satellite** (tel. 833-2031).

Car Hire

New Orleans has plenty of car rental agencies, but before you decide to drive here there are some things you should know. First, walking in the French Quarter is infinitely easier and less time-consuming than driving in the French Quarter. The streets are narrow, some are blocked off for pedestrians and bikers, and those that are not are often jammed with traffic. Parking on the street is difficult; police tow-aways frequent, swift, and costly. Mardi Gras presents special hazards. You need a special pass to drive into the Quarter during Mardi Gras. There is a $100 fine for blocking a parade route, so you need to know where and when the krewes are cruising. Apart from those caveats, driving in New Orleans is like driving in any other big city and you will enjoy the freedom of having a car for excursions into the countryside. Remember that Americans drive on the right.

In order to rent a car you have to be 25 years old with a valid driver's licence (from any country), your passport, and a credit card. Compare prices and check the daily newspaper for special promotional rates. Most of the major car rental companies have outlets at the airport as well as in the CBD. The leading companies are:
Avis (tel. 523-4317)
Budget (tel. 525-9417)
Dollar (tel. 468-3643)
Hertz (tel. 568-1645)
National (tel. 525-0416)

Chauffeur-driven Cars

If you would rather not do the driving yourself, there are companies offering chauffeur-driven cars and minivans. The going rate is $35-$50 during the week, slightly higher on weekends, usually with a two-hour minimum. All the companies listed below offer plantation tours.

A Touch of Class, 907 S Broad (tel. 522-7565) has Lincoln VIP stretch limos, a super stretch, a Rolls Royce, and minibus.

Carey-Bonomolo, 1401 Lafitte Ave (tel. 523-5466) is a 20-year-old company with a wide variety of vehicles. In addition to Cadillacs, Lincoln VIP stretch limos, and Ford sedans, it has a converted London cab.

London Livery, 3037 Royal St (tel. 944-1984) has Lincoln VIP stretch limos, a Rolls Royce Silver Cloud, and 47- and 25-passenger buses.

Chemist (see Pharmacist)

Crime

New Orleans, like all major cities, has a crime problem, most of it drug-related. The precautions you should take are detailed under **Personal Safety.**

Customs Regulations

While aboard ship or on the aeroplane, you will be given a Customs declaration form. Fill out the identification (upper) portion of the form and present it to the Immigration and Customs Inspectors on arrival. Visitors crossing land borders will identify themselves during their oral declaration. All articles brought into the US, including gifts for other

The Crescent City at night, which is when much of it wakes up

persons, must be declared to US Customs at the time you enter. If all the articles you have to declare are entitled to free entry under the exemptions allowed, you need not fill in the reverse side of the declaration form. There is no limit to the amount of money (US or foreign currency), travellers' cheques or money orders that you bring into or take out of the US. However, a report must be filed with US Customs at the time you arrive or depart with amounts in excess of $5,000, or the equivalent in foreign currency. A form will be provided for this purpose. You can bring

into the country, without duty or tax, items for personal use, including photographic equipment. Visitors over 21 may bring one US quart of alcoholic beverages; 200 cigarettes or 50 cigars or 3lbs (1.3kg) of smoking tobacco, or proportionate amounts of each (the State of Louisiana restricts the importation of alcoholic beverages from other US States). In addition to the above exemptions, articles up to $100 in total value for use as gifts may be brought in free of duty and tax if you will be in the US for at least 72 hours and have not claimed this gift exemption in the past six months. This exemption may include up to 100 cigars. Among restricted items are chocolate liqueurs, fruits, seeds, plants and poultry and meat products (eg sausage and pâté). Do not even think about bringing in illegal drugs. If you take medication that contains controlled substances, carry only the quantity normally needed and properly identified. You should also have a prescription or written statement from your personal physician stating that the medicine is necessary for your health.

Domestic Travel
Air Airlines serving New Orleans International Airport include American, Continental, Delta, Eastern, Lacsa, Northwest, Piedmont, Sasha, Southwest, TWA, United, and USAir.

DIRECTORY

Bus Greyhound/Trailways buses (in US tel. toll-free 800/237-8211) connect New Orleans with virtually any place in the continental US. Buses arrive and depart at Union Passenger Terminal, right in the centre of the CBD (1001 Loyola Ave). Cabs are readily available.

In New Orleans, the Regional Transit Authority operates an excellent bus system, as well as the popular St Charles Streetcar (the city's moving Historic Landmark) and the new Riverfront Streetcar. A great way to see the uptown sights, the St Charles Streetcar clangs and rumbles up St Charles Avenue, through the Garden District, past Audubon Park and the Zoo, turns on Carrollton Avenue, and

The new Riverfront Streetcar

terminates at Palmer Park. The Riverfront Streetcar breezes along the Mississippi River from Esplanade Avenue in the lower Quarter to the Convention Center at Julia Street. The Vieux Carré shuttle bus, which looks like a miniature streetcar, scoots through the French Quarter and runs to the foot of Canal Street. Fare for buses and streetcars is 60 cents (exact change required); 30 cents for the CBD shuttle that operates between the Superdome and the foot of Canal Street. Transfers are five cents extra. The RTA puts out a free, colour-coded route map that you can pick up at the New Orleans Welcome Center. It also operates a 24-hour RideLine for information about how to get from here to there (tel. 569-2700; for the hearing impaired, 569-2838).

Rail Amtrak trains (in US, tel. toll-free 800/872-7245) also arrive and depart at Union Passenger Terminal (a place you will not want to hang about in at night). Amtrak trains run between New Orleans and New York, Washington DC, Chicago, and Los Angeles.

Taxis The CBD and French Quarter are usually full of cabs, and you can flag one down in those areas. They don't usually cruise in other areas of the city, but you can telephone for a taxi. Some of the reliable taxi companies are **United Cabs** (tel. 522-9771); **Liberty Bell Cabs** (tel. 822-5974); and **Checker Yellow Cabs** (tel. 525-3311). The 'drop' is $1.10, with $1 for each additional mile.

Ferries Free ferries (bearing cars as well as people) cross the Mississippi River at various points. The ferry from the foot of Canal Street to Algiers is a commute for West Bank residents; a treat for visitors and New Orleanians, who love to go out on their river. There are other ferry crossings from the East Bank to the West Bank at Jackson Avenue in the city and further upriver in plantation country.

Sea If you have enough time and money, you can travel from northern ports (Cincinnati and St Louis among them) in nostalgic style aboard the sleek *Mississippi Queen* or her smaller elder sister, the *Delta Queen* (built in the same shipyard as the *QE 1,* and *QE 2,* and the *Queen Mary*). Luxurious staterooms, dixieland bands, mint juleps, and world-class cuisine are among the considerable attractions as you ease down the mighty Mississippi River. Cruises range from two to eleven nights. The sibling's annual Great Steamboat Race from New Orleans to St Louis recreates the historic 19th-century race between the *Natchez* and the *Robert E Lee*. Before you pack a bag, you should know that a Mississippi River cruise is among the world's most costly voyages. For information, contact the Delta Queen Steamboat Company, 30 Robin Street Wharf, New Orleans, LA 70130-9990 (tel. 504/586-0631; in US, call toll-free 800/543-1949).

DIRECTORY

Arriving by steamboat, you will put in to the Robin Street Wharf, about a 10- or 15-minute taxi ride from the CBD. The passenger terminal is modern and cabs meet the riverboats, but you would not want to stay long in this part of town.

Car Interstate 10 runs across the southern US from Florida to California and right through downtown New Orleans. West of town, Interstate 10 connects with Interstate 55, which runs north-south all the way to Chicago. To reach the downtown area and the French Quarter, take the Poydras Street exit from I-10. The French Quarter exit reads *Vieux Carré*.

The interstates are marked with international designations for restaurants, restrooms, telephones and service stations. In recent years,

The Creole Queen riverboat offers jazz and buffet dinners as well as scenery on its cruises, starting at the Riverwalk Poydras Street Wharf

gasoline prices have been hovering below the $1 per gallon mark. Be sure to keep your rental car documentation safely stashed in the glove compartment.

If you get lost, call AAA Louisiana, tel. 838-7500 Monday to Friday, 08.30-17.00; or 837-1080 after 17.00 and at weekends. Your call will be 'spotted' and you will be told how to reach your destination by car or public transport.

Electricity
110 volts, 60 cycles. US sockets accept plugs with two flat pins. A voltage transformer may need to be bought for electrical appliances of a different voltage, or an

electrical adaptor for those of different connections.

Embassies and Consulates

The Honorary Consulate of Great Britain, 321 St Charles Ave (tel. 524-4180), cannot issue passports or visas. The office is open Monday to Friday 10.00-noon and 14.00-16.00; at other times there is a taped message. For assistance with passports and visas contact the British Consul General, 601 Jefferson Street, Houston, Texas 77002 (tel. 713-659-6270). The Canadian Embassy for the US is based at 1746 Massachusetts Ave, NW Washington DC 20036-1985 (tel. 785-1400).

Emergency Telephone Numbers

Dial 911 in an emergency for co-ordinated aid. Hospital emergency rooms are open 24 hours a day near the CBD and the French Quarter at Tulane Medical Center, 1415 Tulane Ave (tel. 588-5711), and the Garden District at Touro Infirmary, 1401 Foucher (tel. 897-8250).

Entertainment Information

The free weekly newspaper *Gambit* has comprehensive information about the nightclub scene, including which artists are appearing at which jazz clubs; art galleries; theatrical performances; children's activities; and so forth. *Where* is another free publication with up-to-date entertainment news. Each Friday the 'Lagniappe' section of the *Times-Picayune* carries detailed information about upcoming cultural events,

movies, music, etc. 'Overture to the Cultural Season' is a calendar of events available at the Tourist Welcome Center, at Riverwalk, and in many hotels. Events information is available on 566-5047.

Entry Formalities (see Arriving)

Guidebooks

Bookstores in the French Quarter and the CBD carry a plethora of books about New Orleans culture, cuisine, voodoo, history, and architecture, as well as books on how to get from here to there. The *Streetcar Guide to Uptown New Orleans* ($8.95, available in CBD and French Quarter bookstores) is a superb book that takes you by the hand and points out the sights on and around the streetcar route. The Greater New Orleans Tourist and Convention Commission publishes a free self-guided walking and driving tour, available at the New Orleans Welcome Center. *GO* and *Where* are both free monthly magazines, available in almost all hotels, with historical information about the city, as well as listings of art galleries, museums, shops, and so forth. Fodor's and Frommer both publish excellent New Orleans guidebooks, available in CBD and French Quarter bookstores.

Health Regulations

No vaccinations are required to enter the US.

Holidays, Public

Banks and most business offices are closed New Year's

DIRECTORY

Day, Martin Luther King Day (19 January), Inauguration Day (3rd Mon in January, every four years), Mardi Gras (February or March), Lincoln's Birthday (February), Good Friday, Memorial Day (last Mon in May), Independence Day (4 July), Labor Day (first Mon in September), Columbus Day (second Mon in October), All Saint's Day (1 November), Veteran's Day (11 November), Thanksgiving (fourth Thurs in November), and Christmas Day.

Lost Property
Contact the Public Information Office, City Hall (tel. 586-4322).

Fourth of July at JAX Brewery

Money Matters

The rate of exchange fluctuates, and you should check the current rate at the time of your planned trip. It is advisable to exchange at least a small amount of currency before leaving home. In New Orleans, foreign exchange brokers include **Deak International**, 111 St Charles Ave (tel. 524-0700) and **Whitney Bank**, 228 St Charles Ave (tel. 586-7272); and the lobby level at New Orleans International Airport. New Orleans has a 9 per cent sales tax and 11 per cent hotel tax.

Virtually all the hotels and many (but not all) restaurants take American Express, Visa, Mastercard, Diners Club, Carte Blanche, En Route or some combination thereof, as well as travellers' cheques. Eurocard is not widely accepted.

Opening and Closing Times

Banks are open weekdays from 09.00 till 15.00 or 16.00; some stay open later on Friday afternoons. Offices are open weekdays from 08.00 or 08.30 till 17.00 or 17.30; some are open Saturday mornings. Museum and art gallery hours vary greatly, as do shopping hours. CBD department stores are open Monday to Saturday from 09.30 or 10.00 until 17.30 or 18.00. Many French Quarter shops are open every day from 09.00 until 18.00, but hours are often flexible, depending upon how business is. Malls are usually open from 09.00-21.00.

Personal Safety

Most of the crime in New Orleans is drug-related. It is not advisable to stroll around loaded with jewellery and cash. Carry travellers' cheques rather than cash, and leave your valuables in the hotel safety deposit vault. Because the French Quarter is the city's most popular tourist attraction, it is well patrolled and relatively safe, especially during the day. However, at night you should stick to the most active areas (from Jackson Square to Canal Street) and avoid the fringes of the Quarter (Rampart Street and Esplanade Avenue). Louis Armstrong Park should be avoided night and day, except when there are huge crowds going in and out (for Mardi Gras balls at Municipal Auditorium and for performances of opera and ballet at the Theatre of the Performing Arts). Audubon Park and City Park are safe during the day, but both should be avoided after dark. You should go with a group, rather than alone, to visit the cemeteries. Lafayette Square and the area around the Superdome are both bustling and safe during the day, deserted and unsafe at night. Apart from the prestigious Garden District, streets on either side of St Charles Avenue are seedy and unsafe, as are parts of the Lower Garden District.

Pharmacist

The main chains, with locations throughout the city, are

DIRECTORY

Eckerd, **K & B,** and **Walgreen's**. Walgreen's has convenient locations in the CBD, 900 Canal St (tel. 523-7201) and in the French Quarter, 134 Royal St (tel. 522-2736). Two Eckerd's branches are open 24 hours a day: 3400 Canal St (tel. 488-6661) and 4645 Freret St (tel. 899-4017). Eckerd's has a branch at Lee Circle (tel. 586-1234) and in the Garden District, 3401 St Charles Ave (tel. 895-0344).

Places of Worship
New Orleans is America's most Catholic city, but other denominations are also well represented. The following is a brief sampling of the city's numerous houses of worship:

Baptist Churches:
First Baptist Church, 4301 St Charles Ave (tel. 895-8632)
Carrollton Ave Southern Baptist Church, 2528 S Carrollton Ave (tel. 861-8240)
Lakeview Baptist Church 6100 Canal Blvd (tel. 482-3109)

Catholic Churches:
St Louis Cathedral, Jackson Square (tel. 525-9285)
St Patrick's Church, 724 Camp St (tel. 525-4413)
Our Lady of Guadalupe, 411 N Rampart St (tel. 525-1551)
Jesuit Church of Immaculate Conception, 130 Baronne St (tel. 529-1477)

Episcopal Churches:
Christ Church Cathedral, 2919 St Charles Ave (tel. 895-6602)
Grace Episcopal Church, 3700 Canal St (tel. 482-5242)
St George's Episcopal Church, 4600 St Charles Ave (tel. 899-2811)

Lutheran Churches:
Grace Lutheran Church, 5800 Canal Blvd (tel. 482-4992)
Zion Lutheran Church, 1924 St Charles Ave (tel. 524-1025)

Methodist Churches:
First United Methodist Church, 3401 Canal St (tel. 488-0856)
Rayne Memorial United Methodist Church, 3900 St Charles Ave (tel. 899-3431)
Wesley United Methodist Church, 2517 Jackson Ave (tel. 524-8270)

Presbyterian Churches:
Covenant Presbyterian Church, 4422 St Charles Ave (tel. 899-2481)
First Presbyterian Church, 5401 S Claiborne Ave (tel. 866-7409)
St Charles Ave Presbyterian Church, 1545 State St (tel. 897-0101)

Police
The New Orleans Police Department has a force of about 1,300 men and women. There are foot patrols, as well as those mounted on horses and motorcycles. In an emergency dial 821-2222 (367-3535 in Jefferson Parish).

Post Office
The main office of the US Postal Service is in the CBD at 701 Loyola Ave (tel. 589-1112). Windows are open Monday to Friday from 08.00-16.30; Saturday 08.00-13.00. Among the branch offices (which are closed Saturdays) are Vieux Carré, French Quarter, 1022 Iberville St (tel. 524-0072); Carrollton Station, 3400 S Carrollton Ave (tel. 484-6473); World Trade Center, CBD (tel. 524-0033); and Mid-City Finance, 4315 Bienville

Ave (tel. 482-7071).

Senior Citizens

'Senior' usually means men 65 and over; women 62 and over. The Regional Transit Authority offers reduced fares and a special pass for people of 65 and over.

To apply for an RTA ID Card, present proof of age at the RTA Photo ID Center, Maison Blanche, 101 Dauphine St, first floor (tel. 588-2575).

St Patrick's Church, a distinctive feature of Camp Street. Over half the population of New Orleans is Catholic

Many museums and some hotels also offer discounts for senior citizens. In addition, the Golden Age Passport, available free to people over 62 (with proof of age), affords free entry to federally-operated parks, monuments, and recreation areas. The pass can be picked up at any national park that charges admission fees for entry.

Travel Tips for Senior Citizens (US Dept of State Publications 8970) can be obtained by sending $1 to the Superintendent of Documents, US Government Printing Office, Washington DC 20402.

Student and Youth Travel

In order to qualify for discounts, young people must have a student ID. An internationally-accepted student ID is issued by the Council on International Educational Exchange, 205 East 42nd Street, New York, NY 10017 (tel. 212/661-1414). To obtain the ID card, send proof that you are a student (bursar's receipt, for example), proof of age, a passport-size picture, and cheque or money order to the amount of $10 to the Council.

Telephones

To call New Orleans from outside the area, dial area code 504 plus the local seven-digit number. For telephone directory assistance (information) in New Orleans, dial 1-411. For police, ambulance, and fire emergencies, dial 911. Pay telephones require 25 cents except in the case of 911 emergency calls, which are free.

Time

New Orleans is in the Central Time Zone, one hour behind New York and six hours behind Greenwich Mean Time.

Tipping

New Orleans restaurants do not include a service charge in the menu prices, and it is customary to leave a tip of about 15 per cent if you feel the service has been satisfactory. New Orleans waiters are accustomed to receiving a gratuity based on the total amount of the bill, including tax and wine. Tip bellboys $1; skycaps (porters at the airport) and bus porters 50 cents per bag; and taxi drivers 15 per cent to 20 per cent of the fare. Limousine drivers are tipped 15 per cent. In hotels and motels, for a stay longer than one night leave the maid about $1 per night or, on a weekly basis, $5 per week.

Toilets

Most of the major hotels have Ladies' and Men's rooms off the main lobby, and all except the tiniest restaurants have facilities. However, during Mardi Gras most guesthouses, restaurants and bars post signs reading 'No Public Restrooms,' meaning that only guests and patrons are permitted to use the restrooms. The city sets up portable toilets – called Port-o-Sans – along the parade routes and in the French Quarter.

Tourist Offices

Assistance in planning your holiday in New Orleans, as well as useful general tourist information, is available from the **Greater New Orleans Tourist and Convention Commission**, 1520 Sugar Bowl Drive, New Orleans, LA 70112 (tel. 504/566-5011). The New Orleans Tourist Commission staffs a desk next to the Customs Desk at New Orleans International Airport. The **New Orleans Welcome Center** shares an office with the **Louisiana State Information Center** at 529 St Ann St, Jackson Square (tel. 566-5031), and is open every day except Christmas, Thanksgiving, New Year's Day, and Mardi Gras.

Travelling at a lazy pace, to suit the laid-back atmosphere of 'the city that care forgot'

Travel Agencies

American Express Vacations offers a tour that begins and ends in New Orleans, with stops in other Southern cities. Contact them at Box 5014, Atlanta, GA 30302. In the US you can call them toll-free on 800/241-1700. **Domenico Tours** also does tours to New Orleans and a New Orleans/Memphis/ Nashville package: 751 Broadway, Bayonne, New Jersey 07002; in US, call toll-free 800/554-TOUR. Local travel agents who can help you plan trips to other US destinations include **American Express Travel Service**, 158 Baronne (tel. 586-8201); **Thomas Cook Travel**, 201 St Charles Ave (tel. 568-1964); and **Travel New Orleans**, 434 Dauphine St (tel. 561-8747).

INDEX

ACKNOWLEDGEMENTS

The Automobile Association would like to thank the following photographers and libraries for their assistance in the compilation of this book.

AA PHOTO LIBRARY (J. BEAZLEY) 14/5 Cornstalk fence, 17 St Louis Cemetery, 18 Piazza d'Italia, 29 Confederate Museum, 30/1 Old US Mint, 32/3 Audubon Zoo, 34/5 City Park, 36 Haunted House, 74/5 French Market, 76 Fruit seller, 77 & 79 Landmark French Quarter Hotel, 83 Lamothe House, 94/5 Superdome, 96 City Park, 98 Jackson Square, 99 Audubon Zoo, 111 World Trade Center, 123 St Patrick's Cathedral.

R. CALAMIA 90/1 Jazz Brunch.

M. CELENO 114/5 Night Skyline.

NATURE PHOTOGRAPHERS LTD 43 Herring gull (J. Doe), 44/5 Sandwich tern (R. Tidman), 47 Snapper terrapin, 54/5 Swallowtail butterfly (S. C. Bisserot), 48/9 Black vulture, 50 Epiphytes (P. R. Sterry), 53 Yellow Crowned Night Heron (E. A. Janes), 56/7 Grey squirrel (P. J. Newman).

ORLEANS CONVENTION PHOTOGRAPHY 9 Creole cottage, 20 St Louis Cathedral, 23 Gallier House, 24 Longue Vue House & Gardens, 40 Louisiana bayou, 59 Seafood, 66 Commander's Palace, 69 Monday meal, 70/1 Mr B's Bistro, 73 Crescent City, 102 Mardi Gras, 103 St Charles streetcar, 105 Mardi Gras, 110 Café du Monde, 116 Riverfront streetcar, 118 Creole Queen, 120 4th July celebrations.

SHERATON GROUP 80/1 Sheraton Hotel.

SPECTRUM COLOUR LIBRARY 92/3 Paddle steamer, 108/9 Children's playground, 125 Street scene.

ZEFA PICTURE LIBRARY (UK) LTD Cover Paddleboat, 4 New Orleans, 7 Carriage, 12/3 CBD, 26 Oak Alley, 38 St Charles streetcar, 60 Fish dishes, 62/3 Antoine's, 64/5 Café du Monde, 86/7 Preservation Hall, 100/1 Jazz, 106/7 Jazz, 112 Bourbon Street.